Praise for Robert Stephan Cohen and *Reconcilable Differences*

"Robert Stephan Cohen has handled hundreds of big divorce cases, but he thinks yours or mine may not be necessary. *Reconcilable Differences* tells you what you can do to keep from getting to that stage or how to back off from it if you're there already. I'm not contemplating a divorce myself, but I found the book so sound and constructive that I'm planning to send it to several squabbling friends."

—Helen Gurley Brown

"*Reconcilable Differences* is essential reading for couples at all stages of their relationship. Those entering a marriage will profit from Robert Stephan Cohen's profound wisdom. Those feeling stuck and frustrated will find their way back to intimacy, fun, friendship, and sensuality. And those ready to consult with a matrimonial attorney will discover the possibilities of healing and creating an even stronger and more resilient marriage."

—Linda Carter, Ph.D., Director, Family Studies Program,
New York University Child Study Center

"Robert Stephan Cohen's *Reconcilable Differences* is a brilliantly organized plan to save a marriage even before it gets into trouble. His step-by-step approach takes the chaos out of conflict and allows you to approach the situation calmly and compellingly. Required reading for couples!"

—Julie Morgenstern, auth̶ *the Inside Out* and

Out

RECONCILABLE
DIFFERENCES

7 Keys
to Remaining Together
from a Top
Matrimonial Lawyer

ROBERT STEPHAN COHEN

with Elina Furman

ATRIA BOOKS

New York London Toronto Sydney Singapore

While the examples of marital problems in this book are based on real experiences, the author has created composite characters and altered details in order that the privacy of his clients be completely protected.

ATRIA BOOKS
1230 Avenue of the Americas
New York, NY 10020

ISBN 0-7434-0711-3
ISBN 0-7434-0712-1 (Pbk)

First Atria Books paperback printing March 2003

10 9 8 7 6 5 4 3 2 1

ATRIA BOOKS is a trademark of Simon & Schuster, Inc.

Designed by Nancy Singer Olaguera

Printed in the U.S.A.

For information regarding special discounts for bulk purchases, please contact Simon & Schuster Special Sales at 1-800-456-6798 or business@simonandschuster.com

To my wife, Stephanie, whose love and support
inspired me to write this book;
to my sons, Chris, Ian and Nick and my stepson Josh
who constantly remind me how wonderful children are;
and to my daughter-in-law Stephanie and
my new granddaughter Samantha,
who make me smile again and again.

[CONTENTS]

[CONTENTS]

What Divorce Has Taught Me About Marriage

During my 30 years of practicing matrimonial law, I have come to understand that at the heart of every divorce lies one of seven basic marital differences. One or more of these differences affects almost every marriage. But make no mistake, these differences are not irreconcilable.

Part of what contributes to the ever-rising divorce rate are our expectations: More and more people are getting married with the expectation that they will either divorce at some point in their lives or else live happily ever after. Both expectations are formulas for failure, fostered by media images and quick-fix ideas of love and life. Millions of us enter into marriage with self-defeating and unrealistic expectations, and when a marital crisis strikes, as it inevitably does during the course of every marriage, we run to the nearest divorce lawyer for help. That's where I come in.

I can't tell you how many people come into my office with problems that can, with time and effort, be easily remedied. Sadly, many of my clients panic at the first sign of trouble.

My experience has taught me to distinguish between panic and legitimate complaints. There have been many times when I have cordially escorted a client out of my office with instructions to wait a few months before taking further action. Happily, the majority of these panic-stricken clients do not come back. Contrary to popular belief, I'm no stranger to giving the kind of counsel that keep marriages together. Although this means less business for me, I am comforted by the knowledge that I have guided a couple in the right direction.

No matter how many cases I've won or how many settlements I've negotiated, nothing is as satisfying to me as effecting a reconciliation between two people whose union is still fundamentally sound.

In this book you will find tales of many married couples I have observed over the years, some rich and famous and others not. The stories and names have been changed to protect the identities of those involved. I can remember every one of my clients' trials and errors to the very last detail. Cases from ten years ago are as fresh in my mind today as if they happened yesterday.

The book is broken up into seven chapters, each of which details seven reconcilable differences. Each chapter is subdivided into three sections: "Warning Signs" (what to look out for), "Marital Crimes and Misdemeanors" (what not to do), and "Reconciliations" (how to fix it). Each section comes with questions and exercises that will help you get a better idea of how the differences affect your marriage and how to troubleshoot when the going gets tough. Do these quizzes and answer these questions in your mind as you read the book or jot them down in a notebook or a computer file. These seven basic differences can all be resolved in a positive manner, provided you follow the formula that I have outlined and do the work, both internally and with your spouse.

When reading the "Warning Signs" section, keep in mind that in and of themselves, these signs are not cause for alarm. However, if left unaddressed these behaviors can lead to bigger problems, which can be found in each chapter's "Marital Crimes and Misdemeanors" section. This section outlines some of the more serious pitfalls your marriage can fall into. If you find yourself or your spouse committing any of the crimes and misdemeanors outlined, it is very important, perhaps even crucial, that you follow the suggested guidelines in the "Reconciliations" section.

How I've Learned What I've Learned

If someone had told me twenty years ago that I would someday write a book about relationships, I would have laughed. After all, what could a divorce lawyer possibly know about keeping couples together? But over the past thirty years, I have managed to learn a great deal about what draws people together and what pulls them apart.

I have seen people at their absolute worst. When they come through my doors, they can't eat, they can't sleep . . . or they can't do anything but. Life as they know it has come to an end. They will have to acquire a new set of habits and get used to coming home to an empty house. After years of watching my clients pass in and out of my office, their tales of woe ringing in my ears, I did the unthinkable. I, a lawyer, began to feel responsible for their welfare. My role began to change. No longer was I merely obliged to get my clients the best possible conclusion to their failed marriage, I became a one-stop emotional support system: confidante, psychiatrist, and clergyman all wrapped up into one.

The way my clients see it, if they can trust me with their finances and their marital problems, why not with the most intimate details of their private lives? You see, no one wants to admit defeat. People have a way of putting up a brave front to the world, only revealing their greatest fears, grievances, and disappointments to their best friends or psychoanalysts. But even then, they hold something back. In my line of work, that one crucial detail can mean a great deal of money down the drain. You'd be surprised how quickly people reveal their most secret thoughts and experiences when half their net worth is at stake.

I have litigated thousands of cases and represented everyone from teachers to supermodels to real estate moguls. Over the years, one thing has become abundantly clear: Knowing the don'ts is sometimes even more important than knowing the do's. I can't tell you how many times I've sat and listened to clients go on and on about what they could do to make a relationship work. There are times, however, when it's not what you do, but what you don't do that can make the difference.

In all honesty, I, too, have made my share of mistakes. I, too, have committed most of the "don'ts" that I will describe in this book. I, too, have been divorced. It was the most harrowing and painful event of my life. Yet, I credit my divorce with giving me the compassion and insight that I need to help my clients. Who better to help them stand up, brush themselves off, and go on with their lives than someone who's been there and learned from that?

Through my clients' experiences, I have discovered the art of damage control. Whenever I am confronted by a new client with a new set of problems, I ask myself what contributed to their divorce and how other couples can avoid ending up in a similar situation.

And that's exactly what you have to ask yourself: What do you have to do, or rather *not* do, to keep me out of your personal life? How do you avert the relationship detours that lead directly to my doorstep? Well, that's precisely what I am about to tell you. And if that means fewer new clients for me and my colleagues, then that is a chance I'll gladly take. If I learned anything in my many years in matrimonial law, it's that divorce is rarely a solution: Divorce is a life-altering and devastating process that should be avoided at all costs. Take my word for it, because I know what I know.

The State of Our Unions

As a young kid living in blue-collar Brooklyn, New York, the concept of divorce was completely foreign to me. Couples took their vows and never looked back. For better or worse actually meant just that. Only one family in my neighborhood was rumored to be separated, and talking about them was strictly off limits. It was in the most hushed of tones that anybody talked about "divorce."

Of course, marriage was no easier then than it is today. But the trying times of the Depression and World War II made the perils of matrimony seem like heaven on earth. In the war against penury, families worked as tight-knit teams. For instance, I remember how difficult it was to make a decent living back in the day. Instead of breaking up homes, financial problems brought us closer together. Sharing a room or a small meal gave people a sense of community. All was for one, and one was for all, indeed.

But just as people banded together in times of trouble, it seems that the reverse came to be true in times of plenty. In today's consumer culture, everything and everyone has become disposable, from diapers and milk bottles to friends and spouses. Even instant gratification is outmoded in an age when we want everything yesterday.

When I first began litigating, matrimonial law was in its infancy. Not only was divorce still a taboo subject, it also carried none of the financial incentives that it does today. But "breakup benefits" are nothing compared to the overwhelming pain of dissolving a marriage. The stress can result in depression, loneliness, and despair, not to mention physical problems such as high blood pressure and a compromised immune system. All told, divorce is hazardous to your health and well-being, and no amount of property that may be divided is worth the side effects.

I don't have to tell you that the divorce rate is higher than it's ever been. With so many breakups and failed marriages, why are so many people still remarrying, attending relationship seminars, and reading self-help books? In my opinion, it's because more and more people are returning to the basic formula for happiness: committed relationships. No one wants to live alone for the rest of their lives, and those who say they do are lying.

You may balk at the thought of a divorce lawyer preaching the virtues of marriage, but you'd be surprised at just how many of my peers are right now enjoying the fruits of their labor with a partner they love. Just like the general population's search for the perfect mate is undeterred by a high divorce rate, divorce lawyers, too, maintain an optimism that some may say goes against everything we do and see each day. Therein lies the paradox of this book. In spite, or maybe because of, all the lives I've seen torn apart by divorce, I continue to search for answers that will make me a better lawyer, a better person, and, most important, a better husband.

Whether it's incompatible communication styles, money matters, or the seven-year itch, you will undoubtedly recognize yourself in the stories that follow. Just by reading this book, however, you have already distinguished yourself from most of the people who have had the misfortune to come through my office. You have taken the first active step toward improving your marriage and ensuring that our paths never have reason to cross.

You'll also find out:

- why separation never brings people closer together
- why showing interest in your spouse's job can save your marriage
- how too much love in the beginning can cause disaster down the line
- why silence at the dinner table is never golden
- how honesty can sabotage your marriage
- why giraffes never marry elephants
- why certain subjects should forever remain taboo
- how total self-disclosure can ruin your sex life
- why excessive budgeting can be dangerous
- whether two wrongs can sometimes make a right
- why implicit trust and unconditional devotion can spell trouble
- why too much trust can spell trouble
- how to embrace each other's midlife crises
- how family and in-laws can actually *help* your marriage

RECONCILABLE DIFFERENCES

PARALLEL LIVES

As a matrimonial attorney, I have heard many people complain that they have become estranged from their spouses. Dual careers and a lack of commitment to quality time together all factor into what I have come to recognize as the "parallel life syndrome." Many couples who now lead parallel lives began their marriages by taking a keen interest in their partners' lives. As time went on, however, these once happy husbands and wives gradually turned into polite, cohabitating strangers.

Fortunately, many couples have learned the importance of putting each other first. Despite external demands and pressures, they have successfully put each other on top of their priority lists and have become better workers, parents, providers, and people in the process.

One dreary and cold winter day, Bernice, one of New York's top real estate brokers, came into my office. I could see that she was running on empty. Her hair was disheveled and she paced back and forth in my office, refusing to sit down. During the meeting, she expressed concerns about her spouse, Harold, a marketing manager.

"It's almost like we're roommates instead of husband and wife," she fumed. "I come home at around nine o'clock, and we rarely even talk. Fortunately for him, he gets home much earlier than I do, and has usually ordered and eaten whatever take-out he could find nearby. After a few minutes of polite chitchat, he goes to his room and I to mine. I really don't know how we've gotten to this point. We always had so much to talk about. You've probably heard this before, but he was my whole life and it kills me to think about divorce, but sometimes I just don't see any other way. What with our jobs and our crazy hours, we're too exhausted to talk. It's like we don't even know each other anymore."

Just then her cell phone rang. Looking guilty but determined to pick it up, Bernice excused herself by telling me that it could be a client. Her voice was energetic and friendly when she picked up, but it changed a second later when she found out it was her husband. "No, I won't be home in time, Harold . . . Yes, go ahead and order without me. Goodbye."

During the conversation, I began thinking about her situation. I asked her if there was anything she thought could be done to save her marriage, and she replied, "Look, I've tried everything. We just can't seem to communicate like we used to."

I asked her to humor me in an experiment: From the brief exchange on the phone, I had gleaned that Harold wanted her to come home and eat dinner with him. And when I asked her about it, she told me that she was too busy; she had three prospective clients to meet. It was obvious from her distress that she had been working very hard. It was also obvious that she still loved Harold, but didn't know how to fit him into her busy life.

I asked her, "Bernice, what if you canceled your appointments tonight and had dinner with your husband? Would the world end?" At first, she protested, telling me that her husband would just stare at the television while they ate their dinner in silence. But I persisted. "Let's make an appointment on this same day a month from now," I said. "If you're still interested in filing for divorce, come see me and we'll work something out. If something changes, just call my assistant and let her know you're canceling."

She left my office determined to prove me wrong. Despite her protests, I could see that she had become so consumed by her career that she never took the time to really think about how to reconnect with her spouse.

During the first week after our meeting, I couldn't help thinking about Bernice and Harold. Would she come back or call to cancel the appointment? I thought about it constantly for the first week, but as the month progressed other cases and issues came up, and I forgot about the impending appointment.

One day as I was coming back from a tiresome hearing, exhausted and worn out, I returned to my office to see a bevy of messages strewn all over my desk and a reminder from an associate I promised to meet for dinner to go over a case. Instinctively, I picked up the phone to let my wife know I wouldn't be home for dinner. That's when I saw a message with bright red letters; it read "Bernice 4:00 Cancel." The next thing I knew I was climbing into a cab and giving the driver directions to my house.

Since that day, every time my life gets out of control and I feel like I don't have a moment to spare, I think about Bernice and take the short way home.

All of us from time to time need reminders about the role marriage *should* play in our lives. We become so used to our spouse's constant presence that we often forget that we need to be there, too, every step of the way. Bernice had been treating her clients better than her partner. Once she stopped to look around, she discovered that her marriage was more important than closing a deal or impressing a client.

If you're like the majority of people out there, you probably have a hard time seeing your mate for who he or she truly is. It's only natural for our vision to blur with years of familiarity. Like an expired eyeglass prescription, our perceptions get duller and duller with the passage of time. It is only when you consistently update your lenses that you can see the person you married with the clarity they deserve.

Parallel Lives Assessment

As common as this parallel life syndrome is, it is not inevitable. I've seen plenty of couples who have found the strength to recommit themselves to their union. By answering the following questions, you, too, will be one step closer to assessing and fixing any problems that may be creeping into your marriage.

1. How much time do you spend with your spouse? List some activities you engage in together.

   _____

   _____

2. Is the time you spend with your spouse satisfying? Explain why or why not.

   _____

3. How well do you think you know your partner?

   _____

4. List your spouse's favorite food, favorite film, and favorite pastime. Then ask him or her to test your accuracy.

   Food:

   _____

   Film:

   _____

   Pastime:

   _____

5. Does your spouse take the time to tell you about his or her day at work? Yes _____ No _____

   Does he or she listen when you do? Yes _____ No _____

6. Do you take the time to tell your spouse about your plans, interests, and goals? Yes _____ No _____
   Does your partner do the same? Yes _____ No _____

7. Do you feel that your spouse is aware of and supports your goals?
   Yes _____ No _____
   Do you support your spouse's? Yes _____ No _____

8. When you and your spouse plan an outing, do you prefer to go out as a couple or in a group? Why?

   _____

9. Has your spouse ever complained about your absence from home?
   Yes _____ No _____ If yes, how did you respond?

   _____

10. Have you ever complained about your partner's long absences?
    Yes _____ No _____
    If yes, how did he or she respond?

    _____

Parallel Lives: Warning Signs

Let's face it, most marriages don't end with a resounding thump. There's no bolt of lightning, no roll of thunder, no sudden collision. I've seen enough to know that every marriage has its share of telltale signs, and the difference between the people who stay blissfully wed and those who end up on my client list is that those who save their marriages heed the warnings and waste no time in fixing the problems.

Some of my clients prefer to console themselves with the idea that they never saw the big "D" coming, but there are always warning signs along the way. You can ignore them all you want, but open your eyes and you'll see that they are there, crying out for your full and undivided attention.

No one wants to be awakened from a pleasant dream or snapped out of a comforting reverie. No ones wants to stray from a carefully planned-out route. But heeding the warning of a detour sign can prevent you from losing your way and getting so lost that you can't even find the point from which you started.

Any lawyer worth his retainer knows that the courtroom is the last alternative. In fact, most cases never even go to trial because lawyers negotiate settlements beforehand. I am usually able to sense when both parties are willing to compromise. In that case, I will do everything within my power to find a solution that is agreeable to all concerned. The last thing I want to do is waste my time and my client's dollars on a long, drawn-out and, most of all, painful divorce proceeding, a no-win situation for everyone involved. The same thing applies to your marriage: Divorce is the last possible alternative. If you notice a conflict early on, no matter how minor, don't ignore it. Don't vow to deal with it later. Find a solution right then and there, before the problem takes on a life of its own.

Warning Sign #1: Spending Less Time Together

When you first got together, you couldn't live a single moment without one another. You walked around in a daze, cursing the job you previously loved, forgetting to return your best friend's phone calls, and counting the seconds until you could come home and be reunited with the love of your life. Slowly, as you learned more and more about each other, you began looking forward to going to work, going out on the town with your friends, and diversifying your schedule. The idea of a quiet evening at home spent gazing into each other's eyes suddenly lost some of its appeal.

Jeanie and Marvin, a couple who sought my help in settling their divorce, were a classic example of two people who began their marriage on the right foot, traveling together on many occasions and even finding time to eat lunch together three days a week, only to end up in the all-too-common predicament of living parallel lives.

After five years, Marvin's career as a media buyer became so consuming that he had to spend most of his lunches with clients. Soon, he was coming home later than ever, spending weekends engrossed in his work or away on business trips. Jeanie, on the other hand, had given birth to their daughter and was spending her days as a full-time mother. When the couple first came into my office, I asked them what they thought had brought them to this point, and if there was anything they could do to remedy the problem other than divorce. Unfortunately, they had ignored the steadily growing divide far too long and had little hope of a reconciliation.

As time goes on, spending time with your spouse often becomes less and less of a priority. As familiarity sets in, so does complacency. You feel as if you've seen it all and done it all. There's no magic, no thrill of the chase, no mystery. While you might not have "lost that loving feeling," your job resumes its role as your number one priority, and spending time with your wife or husband becomes more of an obligation than a private pleasure.

When Daniel, a psychiatrist and my college roommate, was first dating his ex-wife, Lauren, he was impossible to deal with. She was smart, vivacious, and attractive, but even that couldn't account for Daniel's radical behavior change. He would cut all our phone conversations short, his work was slipping, and he was always late for our meetings. When we finally did manage to get together, Daniel could barely stand to listen to a word I said. And it wasn't as if I was boring him with the minutia of my day at the law firm. I was even going out of my way to talk about those hobbies that were of particular interest to him, subjects that I myself had never particularly cared for. Still, he could not concentrate on the matter at hand. That was how much in love he was.

Fast forward seven years: Daniel was back to his old gregarious self. Indeed, he had become more interested in his profession, his tennis, and his marathons than ever. He was always up for a spontaneous get-together, and was even beginning to show up at gatherings without his wife, whom he would leave behind to take care of their three children. Although he could barely remember the Daniel of seven years past, I could not forget how mindlessly happy he'd been back then. When he came to me to talk about the divorce, he kept bringing up how deeply in love he had been. He couldn't believe how quickly and drastically things had changed.

As I listened to his side of the story, I remember thinking that Daniel's problem was that he'd been *too much* in love in the beginning. He had been so happy and content that he simply assumed that he would always go on being so effortlessly giddy. Because the relationship was so simple, he believed that he would never have to work hard to be happy. In fact, that's precisely what made his happiness back then so thrilling—the thought that it would last indefinitely.

Divorce was not the answer for Daniel. I decided to level with him and told him that there was a 99 percent chance that he would end up in the same position if he remarried or delved into a new relationship. Unknowingly, he had set a pattern that, if allowed to continue, would probably lead all his relationships to the same dead-end. Instead of giving up on his marriage, he needed to pare down his expectations of what he wanted out of a relationship. After all, we can't always be madly in love with the people we love, but we can commit ourselves to making our marriage work, and that is exactly what I proposed that Daniel do.

Like so many of my clients, Daniel never considered the possibility that spending time with his wife would not always be an exciting proposition. He never considered that it would be up to *him* to re-create the simple joy of just being together. I suggested that Daniel adopt this new, proactive approach to his and his wife's happiness, and, if things didn't improve within a year, he could free himself to pursue other options.

Fifteen years later, Daniel is still happily married to his wife. We still see each other from time to time, and on one occasion, I asked him about that day in my office and if he would change anything about his life knowing what he knows now.

He replied, "You know, I think I love my wife more than ever. It's the little things—remembering to call when I promised or coming home on time—that make a big difference. I think the harder we work on staying together, the more we grow to love and trust one another. It's like the effort itself brings us closer together. I can honestly say we've never been more in love, not even when we first met."

Points to Ponder

1. On average, how many hours do you and your partner spend together each week? _____
   If you answered fewer than four, consider making more time for one another.

2. Do you wish that you could spend more time together?
   Yes ____ No ____
   If yes, have you communicated your needs to your spouse?
   Yes ____ No ____
   What response did you get?

Warning Sign #2: Taking Your Spouse for Granted

A related case that came across my desk about ten years back: John, a well-known rock musician, was seeking a divorce from his wife Sabrina, a Manhattan-based supermodel. Their two-year marriage had yielded no kids, a profusion of shared assets, and enough press coverage to make even Dennis Rodman run for cover. It was what one would call a high-profile relationship. The couple couldn't go anywhere without having their whereabouts documented in the pages of *People* or the *New York Observer*. Yet with all their obvious advantages, what initially got them together had much less to do with their glamorous lifestyles than with good old-fashioned love.

Toward the end of their second year, Sabrina was becoming an even more sought-after commodity in the fashion industry, while John's career was feeling the strain of tepid reviews and mediocre sales figures. There wasn't a fashion show Sabrina didn't attend, a magazine that didn't have her on its cover, or a billboard that didn't feature her larger-than-life likeness in some provocative pose. Pretty soon, John was seeing more of Sabrina's pictures than he was of her. Booked from morning to night, with daily flights from England to Paris and back to the United States, Sabrina never denied that her job was important to her. But in all the commotion of her jet-setter lifestyle, she lost sight of her husband and his needs. Sure, they kept in touch over the phone, but that didn't seem to be enough for John, who had begun courting the paparazzi as if they were the royal family themselves.

His friends, who had seen him shun the limelight before, understood where his new desire for visibility came from. John wanted his wife to notice him, even if he had to go through the media to do it. Considering his erstwhile camera-shyness, it was obvious to anyone who knew him that this change had very little to do with his music career. John wanted his wife to come home. Of course, Sabrina couldn't conceive of such a turn of events. One of the reasons the couple had been drawn to each other had been because each thought that the other would understand their fly-by-night existence.

In the end, Sabrina didn't notice how her absence was affecting her husband, and the two ended up in divorce court—and the tabloids.

No two people living in close proximity will ever share the exact same level of satisfaction at any given moment. All of us are individuals with unique thoughts, expectations, and worries. No two people can ever be equally happy at precisely the exact time.

Here's an example. You've just landed a big promotion. You come home ready to celebrate only to find out that your spouse has had a bad day at work. Although you may be as happy as can be with absolutely no complaints to speak of, it's all too likely that your significant other is steeped in an altogether different reality, mulling over some problem or relationship deficit that you'd never even considered. I can't tell you how many times I've rushed to call my wife after a successful court appearance only to be put on hold. It never fails. At the completion of some process that has consumed me for months on end, probability will have it that she's just beginning an important new project at her firm.

You can't change the fact that we're all living in our own, separate worlds. But, short of reading your partner's mind, is there nothing you can do to form a connection?

More likely than not, your partner is always trying to reach out and tell you something. Whether it's through verbal or nonverbal cues, there are always signs that tell you if your partner is feeling neglected or unappreciated. Your job is to recognize those signs before your marriage begins to crumble.

Signs that Your Spouse Needs Attention

Pride, frustration, and anger can keep people from revealing their true feelings of abandonment. Very few individuals will come right out and ask you to stop whatever you're doing and pay attention. Most people will simply assume that if they have to ask for your time and affection it means that you're not really interested in them anymore. You can't tell your spouse you care and expect them to believe it. But you can show them you care: Turn off the TV, focus your attention on your spouse, and voice your concern when you sense that something is wrong. Here are some cues that can clue you in to your partner's loneliness.

Is your spouse:

- suddenly trying to outdo your absence with their own by scheduling more outings and plans with friends?

- taking an overly active interest in your plans and activities?

- canceling personal plans in an attempt to coordinate your schedules?

- trying to overcompensate by planning activities he or she would normally not be interested in?

- taking on many new hobbies?

- complaining of boredom?

Warning Sign #3: Nothing to Talk About

If you've ever eavesdropped on another couple in a restaurant, you can pretty much gauge how long they have been together by the amount of effort they make to hold a conversation. Couples on a first date will usually talk each other's ears off, telling one another everything about their backgrounds, past relationships, and accomplishments. Some couples who've been married a long time can't seem to find anything to talk about. Spending too many meals with a newspaper in one hand and a fork in the other can plague both the happiest and the unhappiest of couples.

While on a business trip in Boston, my colleagues and I decided to go out for a dinner in a five-star restaurant. Although we were having a business dinner, it was the perfect setting for a romantic night out: dim lights, soft music, and some of the best food in the city. Upon arriving, our group was seated next to a couple. At first, I took their silence to be an indication of their comfort level. But it wasn't until the fourth course was completed in silence that I realized something was very wrong with that marriage.

Nothing is sadder than having to watch a couple go through the motions of digesting their dinners in speechless isolation. It's as if you feel partly responsible for their lack of communication. You can't help but think, "God, I hope that never happens to me."

What's left to say after learning everything there is to know about each other? Political views have been discussed; personal ambitions have been talked to death. That leaves only topics like children, a family vacation, or relocation—not exactly the most stimulating way to spend an evening.

People who have been in the same relationship for years are much like old business partners. No matter how hard you try to avoid "shoptalk," it inevitably creeps into the conversation. Much as we try to come up with scintillating conversation that would rival those enjoyed by single people, it seems that we always come up painfully short.

Next time you catch yourself sharing a meal in silence, don't just dismiss it with a wave of the hand. Really think about what it means. Discussing the same topics or not talking at all can be a sign of trouble to come.

Points to Ponder

1. What was the last dinner conversation you had with your spouse?

   _____

2. Do you find that you have more to talk about with your friends than your partner? Yes _____ No _____
   If yes, it could mean that you and your spouse need to rekindle the friendship that first brought you together.

3. Do you enjoy communicating with your spouse less now than when you first got married? Yes _____ No _____
   If yes, you may need to consider bringing up subjects that you had in common in the past.

   _____

Warning Sign #4: No Common Ground

Thomas, the president of a major bank, told me an interesting story about shopping with his soon-to-be ex-wife, Grace. "Although I enjoyed shopping together for common items, I never quite got used to waiting patiently for her in the women's department. During the first year of our relationship, I graciously escorted her to every department store, boutique, and sale, hoping we would be able to spend some time together.

Naturally, she was pleasantly surprised by my willingness to carry her purse as she tried on business suit after evening dress. She had a hard time believing that she had found the one man who loved to shop as much as she did, and, frankly, so did I. As I quickly learned, love makes you do funny things.

"Prior to meeting Grace, an hour of shopping had seemed like an hour and a half too long. But there I was, standing amid the chaos of a sample sale and clutching the sole indication of my immediate purpose—a ladies' handbag—while my wife scoured the aisles, leaving no hanger unturned and no coat unappraised. My single friends even had a name for this phenomenon: 'The Rite of Shopping.'"

Gradually, Thomas became more resentful of his wife's shopping outings. He found that he couldn't put up a false front any longer. Once he admitted to hating shopping and stopped escorting his wife, he found that they were rarely going out together. It was as if her love of shopping had been keeping the marriage going, and without it, the couple rarely crossed paths.

While you don't want to be a carbon copy of your significant other, neither do you want to forget the common interests that brought the two of you together. In the first blush of romance, it can be very hard to gauge whether your new boyfriend or girlfriend really shares your penchant for Monday night football and Saturday afternoon shopping, or whether they're just pretending in order to keep the spark alive.

Time, however, has a way of bringing our real interests to the fore. No longer will you feel obliged to grin and bear it through another day of listening to stock market updates. Never again will you have to trade an extra hour of sleep for a pre-dawn bout of jogging. As the years progress, you will probably become more honest about your true feelings, opinions, and preoccupations.

Hopefully you will find that your sincerity does not rob your marriage of its foundation; that despite all those little innocent lies, the two of you still have the basic principles in common.

Don't let the natural ebb and flow of your shared activities lead you to the point where you're leading parallel lives. Learn to balance the need for independence with emotional availability.

Points to Ponder

1. Do you and your spouse often disagree on what movie to see or what kind of food to order out? Yes _____ No _____ If yes, this may be a sign that you need to learn to compromise.

2. Is planning a vacation together more of a chore than a pleasure? Yes _____ No _____ If yes, consider taking turns making preparations.

3. Do you often do things on your own because of your spouse's lack of interest? Yes _____ No _____ If yes, it could mean that either you need time alone or you are looking for excuses to avoid your spouse.

Parallel Lives: Crimes and Misdemeanors

Outlining the most common mistakes made by couples is probably what I do best. I am in the unique position of hearing about the many pitfalls of marriage straight from the horse's mouth. After years of listening to my clients recite variations on the same theme of disenchantment and disappointment, I have become a virtual catalog of marital dysfunction.

Judging by the response of my own inner circle, I believe that people can turn their married lives around. I can't tell you how many of my friends who visit marriage counselors on a regular basis tell me that my advice has helped them more than any other. They love the fact that I can provide an example or illustration for any problem they are facing.

You can always choose the easy route and let your marriage and family ride on a roll of the dice, but from what I've learned, relationships do not have a way of working themselves out. So remember, to err is human, but to ignore the mistakes of others is just plain reckless.

Crime and Misdemeanor #1: Laying Blame

Couples who are living parallel lives rarely accept blame for the increasingly disjointed state of their union. Husbands or wives who spend too much time away from home, or have somehow lost sight of their mate's needs and desires, can always count on the old "I'm supporting my family" crutch for support. They figure that financial assistance is their primary role in the family, and they often forget about the far more abstract issues of emotional availability and moral support.

However, laying blame on the partner who has less time to make a connection is ill advised. For example, my former client Arlene would constantly berate her hardworking husband, Ed, who worked as an advertising executive, for not spending enough time with their kids. Soon, she began to imagine that every problem—even those that were more her fault than his—was the result of what she termed Ed's "workaholism." This one perceived flaw in her husband's behavior became the marital scapegoat. Even on those occasions when Arlene forgot to pick her daughter up from school or put off informing Ed of some social obligation until the very last minute, she would shake her head in irritation and wonder why her "workaholic of a husband" had to foil all her plans.

Suffice it to say, her behavior did not have the intended results. Instead of spending more time with the children, Ed began to resent his wife and clock even more hours at the office.

Points to Ponder

1. Do you find yourself becoming more and more frustrated with your spouse's absence from home? Yes _____ No _____ If yes, have you tried talking to your partner about changing behavior?

2. Are there times when you knowingly make your spouse feel guilty for being absent? Yes _____ No _____

If yes, you may need to try communicating your needs more directly.

3. Do you complain to friends about your spouse's lack of involvement in family life? Yes _____ No _____
   If yes, you may need to go to the root of the problem and talk to your spouse about making some scheduling changes.

Crime and Misdemeanor #2: Ignoring the Problem

David, a 42-year-old dentist, loved to watch sports and would often tell his wife, Sari, to find other ways of spending her time on Sundays. Eventually, she grew tired of his behavior. Sunday was her husband's one day at home, and she couldn't understand why he would rather watch sports than spend a quiet day with her.

"I saw that Sari was unhappy with what I did with my Sundays," David told me. "But I felt entitled to a little fun. After all, I worked hard all week, and needed some time to unwind and forget about everything. But every time I turned on the TV, I could tell that Sari was extremely disappointed. She would stomp out of the room and give me dirty looks from the kitchen. Finally, I suggested she find some other way to occupy her time. I wanted her to be happy and have something to do. I had no idea she would blow up at me like she did."

Ignoring the problems that come with parallel lives is like pointing a giant fan at an already raging fire—it only exacerbates the difficulties you are facing. Think about it: The fact that you don't pay enough attention to your spouse is the reason you've been feeling so out of touch. Ignoring the fact that you're ignoring your spouse is the ultimate double whammy.

You may think that your husband or wife will eventually find a way to occupy their time. You may even recommend activities like golf or continuing education to help your partner wile away the hours that you're absent. But that is precisely what you don't want to do. This. is what I call "deflecting responsibility."

By encouraging your spouse to find more interests outside the home, you are not only telling your mate that he or she is responsible for your problem, but you are also unknowingly convincing yourself of the very same myth. At this point, the most important questions you can ask yourself are: Why do you want your spouse to find new outside interests? Is it because you want him or her to be happier? Or do you want him or her to find other interests so you can be free to pursue your own?

It is very easy for your spouse to misconstrue your advice to find outside activities. If you have a habit of getting so engrossed in your activities that you wind up ignoring your spouse, your encouragement may be interpreted as just another attempt to "get rid of them"—and that may be accurate.

It's important that you be honest with yourself about your interest, or lack thereof, in spending time with your spouse. After you've carefully analyzed your motives, you will most likely find that your spouse has to decide for himself or herself how much time to spend away from home or pursuing other interests. But don't try to occupy your spouse just so you can have time away. Your spouse may just need to spend more time with you, in which case you have to figure out whether you can fulfill this need, and, most important, whether you want to.

Points to Ponder

1. Do you secretly wish your spouse would make new friends and find new interests? Yes _____ No _____
   If yes, is it because your spouse demands more of your attention than you are prepared to give? Yes _____ No _____
   If no, are you satisfied with the amount of time your spouse spends away from home?

2. Do you feel your spouse has become too dependent on you? Yes _____ No _____
   If yes, consider what you've done to contribute to this state.

3. Have you ever ignored your partner's pleas for attention? Yes _____ No _____
   If yes, you may be responsible for your spouse's dependency. A few kind words or spending some time together will help your spouse become secure in your affection.

Crime and Misdemeanor #3: Accepting Boredom

Routine has a way of settling into the most exciting of lives. By the same token, any marriage can seem monotonous or boring. It's all a matter of perspective. A husband or wife who sees his or her own role as perfunctory won't help create a very solid marriage.

Linda, a young nurse, had been married to Phil, a 44-year-old retail store manager, when she came to me for a consultation. Her main complaint was that she was growing increasingly bored with her husband.

"He doesn't want to do anything," Linda complained. "When he gets home from work, he just reads a magazine or stares at the television. I've tried talking to him about it, but when he asks me what I want to do, I really don't have any idea. My other friends' husbands are always coming up with fun trips and outings, and all Phil can do is sit around and watch life pass us by."

Unfortunately, Linda refused to see how her behavior and lack of initiative contributed to her boredom. She didn't want to focus on herself and take responsibility for the state of her marriage. Instead, she pinned all her hopes on her husband's ability to take control and steer their marriage out of the doldrums. When that plan didn't bear any fruit, Linda blamed her husband for her growing discontent.

The one thing Linda failed to consider was why she wasn't able to take the initiative and come up with some plans for the two of them. When Phil would ask her what she wanted to do, she could have brought a few ideas to the table and let Phil select one he enjoyed. By trying a new activity every week, Linda and Phil could have found a new hobby or interest that they both enjoyed, strengthening their marriage in the process.

Too many of us get caught up in the same "grass is greener" trap that has been the scourge of marriages since the dawn of time. All too often, people blame circumstances such as a slave-driving boss, the kids' tuition, or even the human condition in general—in short, anything and everything to avoid turning the microscope on ourselves, and heaven forbid, discovering a chink in our armor.

Points to Ponder

1. Have you ever surprised your spouse with tickets to a concert or a play? Yes _____ No _____

2. Do you rely on your spouse to plan social activities? Yes _____ No _____

3. Do you believe that boredom is inevitable in marriage? Yes _____ No _____

4. Do you make conscious efforts to spice up your life together? Yes _____ No _____

Crime and Misdemeanor #4:
Belittling Partner's Interests

Next time your partner tells you that he or she is going on a fishing expedition, signing up for an acting class, or anything along these same lines, check whether you display any of the following responses:

1. rolling your eyes

2. looking disinterested

3. asking them what they could possibly see in such a ridiculous pastime

All these behaviors are mistakes, plain and simple.

Acting like you don't care about your spouse's life not only hurts feelings, it can also make your spouse more reluctant to include you in the future.

One client—let's call her Patricia—used to do volunteer work for very important causes in the city. Patricia's husband, Rob, a computer whiz who started an Internet company, didn't take much interest in her philanthropic activities, seeing the charitable events as little more than Patricia's convenient excuse for spending his hard-won money and buying more expensive jewelry. After asking her husband to accompany her to one event after another, only to put up with his surly demeanor all night long, Patricia grew to hate her husband.

"Here I was trying to improve myself and working to organize all these events, and Rob couldn't even muster up a little enthusiasm," she explained. "All I wanted was one kind word. He never even asked me one question about what I did. It showed me that he didn't care about me, so I stopped caring about him."

Soon she met someone new, someone who appreciated her commitment to bettering the world. Shortly thereafter, we were discussing the terms of her divorce in my office.

I'm not suggesting that you should take an interest in your spouse's pastimes simply to ward off unwanted suitors. But you should make a concerted effort to validate your spouse's lifestyle. Even if you can't possibly understand your spouse's passion for a certain pursuit, accept it as you would everything else about him or her. Asking your partner questions about outside interests and nodding politely as he or she talks is the best way to help your mate feel appreciated. Eventually, you might even form the type of bond that will enable you to recognize some of your own passions.

Points to Ponder

1. How do you feel about your spouse's outside interests?

   _____

2. Do you enjoy having time alone or resent being away from your spouse?

   _____

3. If your feelings are negative, have you expressed these thoughts to your spouse? Yes ____ No ____

Crime and Misdemeanor #5: Compromising Your Identity

Like belittling or sabotaging your spouse's activities, trying to push your way into his or her plans can also backfire. Spending time together is critical, but so is spending time apart doing things you enjoy on your own. When you find that you're insinuating yourself into your mate's plans or tagging along on outings with friends, take it as an indication that you are feeling threatened by their independence.

People confuse independence with lack of love. Instead of giving a husband or wife the freedom to do as they choose, the codependent personality can become controlling and bothersome. These insecure individuals will often go to great lengths just to make sure that their spouses are not left to their own devices.

A client of mine was the publisher of several important literary magazines. Roger was a scholarly fellow, with a keen ear for the English language and a keen eye for classic, tailored looks. His marriage to Amanda was one that few of his friends understood. She was a professional fitness trainer, and led an extremely active lifestyle. Roger, on the other hand, was the kind of guy who turned up his nose at the idea of breaking a sweat. Still, he was very much in love with his wife, and wanted to make her happy.

"In the beginning of the relationship, I went out of my way to accompany her to the gym. I hated the idea of working out, but wanted to make an effort on her behalf. Amanda wasn't fooled. I couldn't curl five pounds or even run on the treadmill for more than five minutes. I would also complain and get on her nerves the entire time we were there. I was miserable, and so was she. She felt that she couldn't do anything without me tagging along. It was Amanda who realized that things just weren't working out between us. No matter how hard we tried, we just couldn't find enough common ground to make it work."

The flip side to this equation portends an equal amount of marital discord. Although you may avoid the mistake of tailing your husband or wife on their various excursions, you might find yourself pressuring your partner to become overly involved with your lifestyle. Don't overstep the bounds between persuasion and coercion. Undue pressure can actually make your spouse even more hesitant to join in. Consider this the next time you try to drag your partner out to see friends he doesn't particularly like or movies she has no desire to see. Think about the good time you'll have without that sourpuss at your side, and give both your spouse and yourself a break.

Points to Ponder

1. Have you ever tried to convince your spouse to join you in an activity? Yes _____ No _____
   If yes, how often does this occur?

   _____

2. How often do you change your plans in order to spend time with your spouse?

_____

3. Have you ever feigned interest in an activity just to be with your spouse?

_____

Parallel Lives: Effecting a Reconciliation

Now that you know what to look out for and what not to do, it's only fair that I share some of the tips I've picked up through the years. Spending more time with your spouse and improving the quality of that time is what we all ultimately strive for. Although my clients have a lot to teach us about what not to do, their stories do include some very important strategies for making marriage work.

Reconciliation #1: Schedule Time

Most people think that love should always be magical and spontaneous. They loathe the concept of scheduling private moments with their loved ones for fear that this will suck the romance right out of their marriage. Then again, life can move so fast that if you don't set aside time for yourself and your loved ones, no one will bother to remind you about what's truly important—the reason you're working so hard to begin with. Fortunately, it doesn't take an entire community to keep a couple happy. All you need are two people who are willing to put forth just the right amount of effort.

In the beginning, letting your relationship take its own course is important, but now that you have committed yourself to one another there should be some element of organization—a method to the madness if you will. Say you decide to surprise your spouse with a lunchtime picnic in the park. You arrive at her office with all the accoutrements, only to find out that her boss has just set a tight deadline that will keep your spouse glued to her desk for the rest of the day. Calling first may not sound like the mantra for romance, but you'd be surprised at just how important it is to your relationship.

Janine, a 37-year-old senior analyst at a busy Manhattan investment bank was struggling with the demands of her job and her marriage. Her career didn't leave much time for anything else. On an average day, she would arrive at work at 7 A.M. and stay until 10 P.M. Her marriage almost fell apart under the strain of her busy schedule.

After some thought and consideration, Janine decided to take a more proactive and involved approach to her marriage. Instead of using her lunch hour to network with colleagues or take out clients, she now makes sure to set aside at least two lunches each week for her husband. After a while, this behavior became second nature and the couple became reinvested in their life together.

She now takes special pains to schedule time to see a movie, go to dinner, or to leave work earlier in order to spend time with her husband. Janine used to think that having her assistant schedule time for her and her husband was cold and unloving. But now she understands it's much better than not spending any time together at all.

Exercise: Not Enough Time?

The first step to scheduling time for your partner is simple: Keep track of how much time you spend on every activity. If you've ever wondered where did the time go, you will no longer be left in the dark. Once you've calculated how much time you spend on routine daily activities, try to determine what you can do to shorten that amount of time. Then, devote that extra time to your spouse. Just thirty extra minutes a day can amount to a world of difference in the quality of your marriage. Consider:

- How many hours do you spend watching TV each night? _____

- How long do you surf the Web each day? _____

- How long do you spend at the gym? _____

- How much time do you spend on the phone? _____

Now, how many of these hours can you take from these activities and devote to your spouse? _____

Reconciliation #2: Start with a Subtle Gesture

The most happily married people understand that they shouldn't get worked up over every little thing. However, that's not to say that little things don't matter when it comes to making your spouse happy. As the saying goes, God is in the details, and little things add up to a lot when you're trying to do something nice for your spouse.

Doing one small thing a day can make all the difference. I'm not talking about grand displays of affection or buying expensive gifts. It's subtle gestures, such as calling in advance if you're going to be late or offering to pick up dinner, that can bring the two of you closer together.

A few years back, I was working on a case where the opposing counsel happened to be an especially tough advocate. When the two of us met, she wouldn't budge an inch toward a settlement. I couldn't believe it, but it actually seemed as if she wanted to go to court. Just as it looked as if she were about to pop a vein on her forehead, her executive assistant knocked on the door and informed her that her husband was on the line. I expected her to snap at her assistant the same way she'd been snapping at me throughout our meeting. Instead, her whole face lit up. Their conversation was brief, but I overheard her telling her husband that she loved him and couldn't wait to see him.

"Oh," I thought, "newlyweds." As it turned out, however, they had been married twenty-five years. By the time she was through with the call, both of us had calmed down so much that we reached an agreement within fifteen minutes, and then spent the rest of the meeting talking about our families. The smallest thing like telling your significant other "I love you" when you're with a client or just taking the time to talk to your spouse can make a big difference in how you feel about yourself, your marriage, and even the opposing counsel.

Reconciliation #3: Renew Your Vows Every Day

Just because you're committed to your partner on paper doesn't mean that you have to stop at that. Emotional commitment is just as important as the legalese that binds your union. A wedding ring is a good way to proclaim your love to the world, but I've seen too many couples lose sight of their vows with the march of time. "I vow to honor, respect, and . . ." oh, you know the rest, right?

A false sense of security can lull anyone into forgetting their vows and the reasons they married their partner. You don't have to be desperately unhappy to take your spouse for granted. On the contrary, sometimes being too content and self-satisfied can hinder you from exerting the effort necessary to keep your marriage running smoothly.

Staying committed to your relationship—mind, body, and soul— takes a considerable amount of work. After all, most people's vows did include the phrase "for better or worse." Imagine how simple marriage would be if the times you shared were always joyful. There would be no divorce. The difference, however, between the couples who get divorced and those who stay married is not that the latter have been lucky enough to come across nothing but happy days, but that the former have given up on working things out.

Reminding yourself of why you fell in love with your spouse can be all it takes to keep your liaison from falling into the doldrums. Think back to your first date. Try to reflect on what it was about your mate that first got your attention, or think about something they did that made you realize you were in love. Was it the way they laughed, something they said, or just the way they looked at you? Although you think your spouse may have changed over the years, there's still a part of them that wants to be the person you fell in love with. By holding that picture in your mind day after day, you will have encouraged them to return to the past and recapture some of the magic of your relationship.

Points to Ponder

1. What first attracted you to your spouse?

   _____

2. Try to remember your first kiss. How did it feel?

   _____

3. When did you first realize that you had fallen in love?

   _____

4. Why did you decide to get married?

   _____

Reconciliation #4: Role Reversal

No doubt, many of you have heard of therapists who implement role play into their sessions with clients. This practice involves the partners switching roles and mimicking each other's behavior and speech patterns. When the fifty minutes are up, the couple returns to their usual lives with a little bit of insight into how they are perceived by their spouses.

It is my belief that role reversal can be that much more effective if it is carried out on a regular basis. If you ever hope to fully appreciate one another, you will have to step into each other's shoes at least once a month. Although your company will probably not institute a "Bring Your Spouse to Work Day" anytime in the foreseeable future, you can still find ways to help your partner understand your lifestyle. For instance, if you are an accountant, you can help your husband or wife by taking him or her through your day at the office. Bring home some work so the two of you can work on it together. If you're in customer service, write a mock script of your average interaction and ask your spouse to play a role in your life drama.

David, a national sales manager for a major men's magazine, was required to travel at least three times a month. He was single when he accepted the position, and enjoyed the idea of traveling. But it wasn't until he met his wife, Ann, that his job became more of a liability than an asset.

While he traveled around the country, missing his family and attending one stuffy business lunch after another, Ann was home taking care of their two sons. They tried to appreciate the difficulty of each other's positions. Unfortunately, David couldn't get over his envy of Ann's ability to spend as much time as she wanted with their boys, while she couldn't conceive of the fact that his life wasn't all about a burning passion for sales, fascinating meetings with interesting people, and a love of travel.

David knows now that had he tried to walk a day in Ann's shoes, and vice versa, their marriage could have fared better. It seems so simple now, but back then he couldn't have imagined that doing something so minor could have made such a huge impact. Sure, role reversal may be a bit of an inconvenience, but it's nothing compared to the ordeal of suddenly having to face your life alone.

Points to Ponder

1. Try to pinpoint a challenge that your spouse deals with each day.

   _____

2. What skills does your partner need to excel at his or her job?

   _____

3. How well would you cope if you were stuck with your spouse's workload?

_____

Reconciliation #5: Go Back to Just the Two of Us

If you're like most people, chances are that over the years your marriage has gone from "just the two of us" to "us against the world." With nary a single carefree moment, couples are forever united in the common purpose of putting out fires and dodging bullets. It seems as though the lives we lead resemble a battleground more than the lovers' paradise we'd anticipated in adolescence. Whether it's attending a parent–teacher conference at school, dealing with difficult in-laws, or trying to keep your bank balance out of the red, the two of you are always trying to protect your way of life. The question is: What are you doing to protect your marriage?

Being there for one another in times of trouble is important, but so is having an enjoyable common purpose. And by that I don't mean sharing couch space and staring at the same large-screen TV. I can't tell you how important it is to schedule activities with your spouse that are enriching as well as entertaining. A couple I've been friends with for years swear by their daily ritual of power walking. Both had been out of touch and out of shape for years. What with working nine-to-five and tending for the kids, they had tremendous difficulty making time for one another. Today, they swear by their ritual, claiming that it has dramatically improved their marriage and their health.

Cooking, dancing, sports, exploring the great outdoors . . . you decide in what way you would prefer to spend your time. But by all means, share something you love to do with the person you love.

If there's ever been a guaranteed recipe for a successful marriage, learning to share would be it.

Exercise: The Friendship Factor

1. I know and can prepare my partner's favorite food.
   True _____ False _____

2. I know who my partner's best friend is. True _____ False _____

3. I know who my partner likes least at work. True _____ False _____

4. I know what qualities my partner looks for in a friend.
   True _____ False _____

5. I know what book my partner values most. True _____ False _____

6. I know what stresses my partner is feeling right now.
   True _____ False _____

7. I know when something is bothering my partner.
   True _____ False _____

8. I know my partner's three favorite record albums.
   True _____ False _____

9. I know which family members my partner likes most.
   True _____ False _____

10. I know what career my partner would choose if money wasn't an
    issue. True _____ False _____

If you answered "true" to most of these statements, then you are probably equipped with a good understanding of your spouse and have a solid friendship on which to build a secure marriage. Answering "false" to as few as four of the above statements can mean that you're not making enough of an effort to get to know your spouse. A simple solution would be to ask your spouse more questions and then really listen to the answers.

Parallel Lives: Closing Argument

Staying connected can be the biggest challenge a couple has to face. With so many elements conspiring to keep us apart, keeping a marriage strong can often seem like a superhuman feat. But keeping your life from falling on parallel tracks is not as hard as it appears. Sometimes, just paying attention is enough to keep your marriage from falling apart.

By staying conscious of potential pitfalls, you will be in a unique position to stop problems before they begin. Remember: Spending less time together is not in and of itself an indication that your marriage is in trouble provided that the time you spend together is happy and conflict-free.

COMMUNICATION

How do we communicate with one another? How honest and truthful are we about our feelings? How well do we use conflict to improve our relationships rather than destroy them?

In my many years of practicing law, I have found that poor communication skills are a major contributor to divorce. Most couples who divorce have never been able to establish a direct line of communication between one another's hearts. But good communication skills can be developed, even in marriages that have lagged in this area. It's never too late to start. In fact, healing can begin almost immediately as long as both partners are willing to acquire the kind of communication skills that keep marriages together.

An old colleague of mine, Walter, once told me this story: "I don't usually prepare my opening statements at home, but I was running late one morning and had no other choice. Grueling work, but I had finally done it. I had composed what I thought was the perfectly crafted argument. And just as I was polishing off the final sentence, my wife Penelope came barging through the door.

"The interruption was by no means welcome. I was just about to cap off what I considered one of the best closings of my career, and had lost my train of thought. So when I looked up at my wife with the intention of letting her know exactly how I felt, I was surprised to find her looking even more displeased than myself."

It turned out that Walt's wife was angry with him for not picking up the phone. Apparently, it had been ringing off the hook for the past five minutes, and he had been too engrossed in his work to hear it. Walter's first reaction was to argue with her. After all, she had only been interrupted from her shower, and he had been interrupted from his work on an important case.

Walter felt self-righteous and was determined to get his way.

"But before I could lash out, something came over me. I had just spent an hour using reason and logic to make my argument more persuasive. As I tried to figure out how to best present my case to the judge, emotions had never entered into the picture.

"That's when it occurred to me: Why not take the same strategy I used in the courtroom and apply it to my marriage? Instead of letting my bruised ego and anger distort my argument, I decided to use reason and logic. And what do you know, it worked!

"After I explained what had happened, how I had almost finished my statement when she rushed into the room, Penelope's expression relaxed considerably. I then went on by appealing to her own work ethic, reminding her of how she hated to be interrupted when she was busy working on an account. Once I had made my statement in a calm and rational manner, my wife was no longer upset. If anything, she sympathized with how hard I had been working and brought in a fresh cup of coffee as a gesture of goodwill. The strong connection between my communication style in my marriage and in the courtroom could no longer be denied."

Walter's story contains one of the most important communication lessons I have ever come across: Truth and justice play as important a role in a marriage as they do in a courtroom. In court, you have to back up your arguments with cold, hard facts or suffer the consequences of defeat; the only thing that matters is what you can prove and how you go about proving it. The same thing goes for your marriage. It is very important how you present your case to your partner.

But in marriage as well as in court, a willingness to settle can be more important than "being right."

Communication Assessment

In my many years of experience working with couples who are on the brink of divorce, I have learned just what is needed to improve communication. I have seen couples' lives ravaged by arguments, denial, and blame. Yet, I have also seen relationships rebuilt with empathy, sensitivity, and compassion. Simply understanding that you need to work on your communication skills is crucial to mending the wounds that a lack of communication inevitably creates. As you answer the following questions, be honest with yourself and pay special attention to whatever the questions themselves bring up.

1. How often do you argue with your spouse? What are the arguments usually about?

   _____

2. How well do you resolve conflict? Do you stay angry for long periods of time?

   _____

3. Do you feel that you can tell your partner anything? If not, what can't you say?

   _____

4. Have you ever agreed with your spouse just to avoid a conflict? How did that make you feel?

   _____

5. Have you hidden something from your partner, fearing he or she will become angry with you? What would happen if you stopped hiding?

   _____

6. Do you look more to your friends for advice than to your spouse?

_____

7. Do petty squabbles have a way of escalating into mean-spirited fights with accusations and personal insults? How does this usually occur?

_____

8. Have you ever resorted to personal insults while arguing with your partner? Who usually says what—and why?

_____

9. Do you regularly compliment your partner on his or her achievements? How does your partner respond?

_____

10. Are you communicating more now than when you first got married or vice versa? In what ways—and why?

_____

Communication: Warning Signs

Warning Sign #1: Fighting Too Much

When two people share one roof, one bathroom, and one closet, countless difficulties and a total lack of privacy are all but inevitable. So, it's a fact of life that couples will and do quarrel. The real problem, however, arises when there are more arguments than good times, when a couple gets so habituated to communicating through shouting matches that they forget what it feels like to have a peaceful conversation over dinner. It's a simple matter of checks and balances: When bad times begin to outweigh the good, it's a warning sign that serious communication problems are developing, problems that could lead to divorce.

A certain degree of conflict is good for a marriage. Heated discussions can help you communicate ideas you would otherwise have kept to yourself. Constructive arguments and impassioned debates can spice up a marriage, helping you to iron out your thoughts and retain your independence within a tight-knit relationship.

But what happens to a couple when fights become the norm and peace becomes the exception? I see the outcome of that situation every day. When a new client comes into my office, one of the most frequent complaints I hear is: "We just can't seem to talk like normal people. Everything becomes an argument. So we've stopped talking altogether."

When I hear that, I know that the problems in that marriage have gone unaddressed for far too long. But I also know a solution can often be found. Counseling can do a world of good, and you'd be surprised at how often I find myself recommending just that. But after living in a minefield of accusations and insults, most of my clients are too exhausted to strive for anything more than a quick fix to a persistent problem.

The question, then, is how do you know if your arguments are constructive or destructive? How do you know if they will eventually lead to the dissolution of your marriage? In order to find out, you'll first have to ask yourself: "What do I and my spouse fight about?" In a constructive argument, you debate world events and which candidate should be elected president. In a destructive argument, you argue about who should do the dishes and who should pick the kids up from school.

The distinction is critical. In my experience, people who argue about impersonal matters like politics and current events often view each other as playful competitors. They feel energized by their debates, instead of drained and exhausted. People who often argue about personal matters view each other as villains and victims. They feel enervated by their persistent arguments.

George, an electronics engineer, and his wife Wendy, a publicist, were divorcing after three years of marriage. Both were in their early thirties, and were ready to start a family. "It was right around that time that we began bickering about everything, from who would leave work to where we would live," George explained. "And it wasn't just isolated fights with a resolution; our fights could sometimes go on for days, with both of us giving each other the silent treatment. Finally, we had to admit that something was wrong in our relationship. Maybe we were rushing into starting a family. I knew that our constant arguing had more to do with our doubts about the future than anything else."

Couples who constantly bicker about the details of their everyday lives are trying to express a general dissatisfaction with the marriage. They pick at little things for the sole purpose of drawing attention to the relationship, basically saying, "I am not happy with the way things are going, and it's all your fault."

If this is the case, and the channels of communication don't open up soon, the marriage may still trudge along, but all the couple's therapy in the world isn't going to be enough to salvage the love that once brought two people together. If you are in a relationship like that, spend some time thinking about the answers to the following questions.

Points to Ponder

1. How frequently do you quarrel with your spouse? If it's more than three times per week, take time to consider what you are fighting about and what is really important to you.

    _____

2. How quickly do you resolve the conflict? If you stay angry for days, or even weeks, you may want to pay careful attention to the reconciliation section at the end of this chapter.

    _____

3. What types of issues do your arguments revolve around? If
   the conflict often turns personal, make a point of
   dissolving conflicts before they erupt into a serious battle
   of wills.

   _____

Warning Sign #2: Drastic Shift in Personality

There's no way around it; marriage defines who we are. It colors the way
we see the world, and alters every aspect of our lives. In some cases, this
can be good. If both partners communicate and share their feelings
openly, one can begin to feel optimistic about the world in which they
live, and actually become better people by virtue of being married.

Still, there are many situations in which a struggling marriage can
have a negative impact on one's life. When two people who live together
are forever at loggerheads, they can begin to anticipate arguments from
everyone they meet, become sullen and closed-off with their friends,
and wind up expecting the worst from life in general.

Nancy, a pert boutique owner in her late thirties, was seeking a
divorce from her husband of over ten years. Hers is an interesting story,
and one that thankfully has a happy ending.

Nancy met Bill, an accountant for a large firm, at a wedding she
attended with another date. They were drawn to each other instantly,
but both were dating other people at the time. Nancy told me that Bill
pursued her relentlessly. Finally, after breaking up with his then girlfriend, Bill asked Nancy to give him a chance and she did. They were
married a year later.

"I was always the life of the party, and Bill, being so quiet and
moody, loved that about me," Nancy explained. "He would introduce
me to all his friends and coworkers. He loved that I made a good
impression on them and could charm the people he needed to impress.
But after a few years, I could tell Bill's attitude had changed. I think he

got tired of me being so outgoing and friendly. I think he wanted to have some of the attention for himself. But that was just my nature. I run a boutique and have to be friendly. Most of my customers come from word-of-mouth, so personality is everything.

"Bill and I started fighting more and more. He resented my happy outlook on life, especially since his job wasn't going as well as he'd have liked. But all Bill needed was a positive attitude, and when I would tell him so, he would think I was saying he was a negative person, which wasn't true at all.

"Eventually, after fighting for the past three years over this and that, my own take on the world began to change. I was no longer excited by working at the shop. I even avoided my friends because I was always in such a dour mood. Fighting with Bill had begun to affect my outlook on everything. I wasn't happy. It was my sister, who was always very honest with me, who finally alerted me to how I had changed. Of course I hadn't noticed; the change had been so gradual that I didn't even realize what was happening until it was too late."

I didn't tell her at the time, but I couldn't disagree more. It seemed to me that Nancy had a realization and acted a little too drastically. She was completely in the right to be upset, but I was confident that she and Bill could work things out provided they learned to communicate. When I asked Nancy if she had talked to Bill about the change in her personality, she looked surprised that I would even ask such a thing. "After all," I said, continuing to press my point, "it was precisely the lack of communication that got you into this boat in the first place."

After three months, Nancy phoned to thank me. She and Bill had talked things out. Realizing that he had almost lost his wife, Bill made a concerted effort to cooperate with Nancy on changing not only the way they fought but what they fought about. And although she admitted that she still harbored some doubts about the future, she was satisfied with the effort Bill put forth.

A drastic shift in one partner's personality is almost always accompanied by an equally drastic shift in the couple's love life. The quality of our lives and the state of our marriages go hand in hand. Finding that you've become more tense, anxious, and depressed since the beginning of your relationship? Chances are you're not getting the most out of your marriage, and your communication style is the most likely culprit.

Points to Ponder

1. Have you, or any of your friends or coworkers, noticed a change in your personality since your marriage? Can you think of anything in your relationship with your partner that may have caused it?

   _____

2. Has your relationship with your spouse put a damper on your outlook on life? If yes, do you think you could communicate your dissatisfaction in a constructive manner?

   _____

3. Was your overall mood and outlook better when you first got married? If yes, do not prolong the inevitable: Talk to your spouse and make sure he or she is aware of these changes.

   _____

Warning Sign #3: Overreliance on Friends

What can you say about friends? If you happen to have a few good ones, you're luckier than most. They're there for you when you need them, both in times of trouble and in times of joy.

I'm sure there have been plenty of times when a marital spat has sent you running for the wise counsel of a good friend. We've all been there. I can't say how many times I've helped my struggling married friends by acting as an intermediary or by just listening and helping them talk through their problems. Still, there are times when looking to your friends too much could be a problem in itself.

David, a young business consultant, called me to discuss divorcing his wife of three years. Kelly, he told me, had just received her M.A. in social work, and was planning to work with underprivileged children. From the way he described her, she seemed like the ideal woman: smart, caring, and loyal. The one drawback, according to David, was that Kelly was too demanding, always insisting that they spend more time together.

"When I married Kelly, she knew I loved going out with the boys, especially my best friend, Pete. We've known each other since high school, and I think she resents how close we are. I think she thought that once we got married, I would stop spending so much time with Pete. But I would never think of it. Whenever I have a problem, whether at work or in my personal life, I could count on my friend's advice to help me through it. I don't think Kelly understands me as well."

"Have you tried to talk to Kelly about this?" I inquired.

"Not really, but when I tell Pete about my problems with Kelly, he always sees my point of view."

I realized that Kelly was probably resentful—and rightly so—of David's relationship with his friends. So when David came back for a follow-up visit, I had a serious heart-to-heart with him about neglecting to confide in his wife. In fact, I even ventured to say that if he confided a little more and treated his wife more like he did his friends, he would probably find that she would be much less resentful of his outside friendships. David thought about it and promised to give it some thought. While that one bit of advice may not have helped the couple settle all their problems, they have since decided to stay together.

Going to outside parties for help once in a while is all well and good, but if you find that you're seeking their counsel with increased frequency, then it's time to face the possibility that something may be very wrong with the way you're communicating with your partner.

How many times have you sought your friends' advice in the past month? Has the amount increased during the time you've been married? If so, then you may need to start articulating your feelings to the one person who can really benefit from your feedback: your spouse.

Warning Sign #4: Holding Long Grudges

A memory is a wonderful thing. But there are times when our memories are responsible for divorce. How many times has one painful memory triggered a protracted argument between you and your spouse? You may be having the time of your life, enjoying a romantic interlude even, when, out of the clear blue, your mate says something that takes you back to a time when you were in the mood for anything but love.

It's only a matter of time till that memory translates into an argument, and you're right back where you started from. Holding grudges and refusing to let go of the past is something that can take a toll on any marriage.

Unforgiving attitudes can ruin the best of relationships, but never has the hazardous effect been so clearly illustrated to me as when my wife, Stephanie, and I attended a dinner party given by our friends, John and Glenda. When we arrived, our hosts greeted us warmly at the door, looking every inch the happily married couple. All through dinner they laughed at each other's jokes, sang each other's praises, and went out of their way to help out whenever possible.

Everyone was laughing and having a great time when, out of nowhere, Glenda stormed out of the room, wreaking havoc in her wake by dropping the wineglass she'd been holding.

A few weeks prior to the dinner engagement, my wife had told me something about John and Glenda that turned out to be the cause of the turmoil. Glenda had been very excited to celebrate her birthday. She had been hoping John would take her on a trip or do something special and she had been anticipating it for months. When John didn't bring anything up on the subject, Glenda just assumed he was planning to surprise her, which made her anticipation mount all the more. So on the day of her birthday, she waited for something to happen. Unfortunately, John had forgotten all about it, and it wasn't until the evening of her birthday that Glenda confronted him. It was too late for John to do anything about it, save make a lot of apologies and promises.

The birthday had come and gone, but from her reaction at the dinner party four weeks later it was obvious that the wounds hadn't healed. John made a jocular reference to his habit of forgetting a friend's birthday, and although his friend didn't mind being so slighted, Glenda couldn't take the oversight with the same equanimity. She had been furious with John for a month for forgetting her own birthday, and now she was even more furious that he seemed to be making light of it.

Racing after Glenda into the kitchen, John seemed genuinely confused and absolutely appalled. He had made every effort to repair the damage of forgetting his wife's birthday by buying her a necklace that soon became the envy of all her friends and taking her on a vacation to Hawaii. After making such a concerted effort, he was shocked to find out that all of his efforts were in vain. He was even more shocked to find out Glenda was just as angry with him as ever.

John wasn't entirely at fault in this situation. Although he forgot his wife's birthday, Glenda's reaction created a silent barrier between her and her husband. She put up a happy front but was still feuding with him beneath the surface.

Forgiveness is an important part of living together in harmony, but forgetting is not the same as forgiving. Sometimes we choose to forget about some minor infraction for the good of the relationship, but forgiving means truly letting go of resentment. If you find that letting go of your grudges has become too difficult, you may have to get to the real problems that are intensifying your resentment. If you cannot let go of the resentment, think about what you may *really* be holding on to.

Points to Ponder

1. Have you ever been rewarded for holding a grudge with presents and extra affection? If yes, did you feel better after receiving the gifts or worse for having gotten them as an afterthought?

2. Have you ever told your spouse you've forgiven him or her even when you were still angry? If yes, make an effort to be up-front about your feelings so the two of you can move toward solving the problem together.

    _____

3. Has your partner ever made you feel guilty by bringing up past mistakes? If yes, do not ignore the problem in hopes that it will go away. Try to resolve the issue immediately when it comes up.

    _____

Exercise: Four Steps to Forgiveness

The act of forgiving is a lot more complex than it appears. Sometimes when we think we've forgiven the offending party, we've simply brushed the problem under a rug. In fact, the same issues can continue to creep into your life unless you take the following steps to make sure that your forgiveness is real.

1. *Take charge:* Explain to your spouse what he or she did wrong, and express exactly what you need: an apology? a promise not to do it again? an explanation of why they did it in the first place? Be very clear that you need this in order to grant forgiveness.

2. *Express your pain:* Forgiving can be a lot easier if you talk about your feelings of pain. Not only will your spouse fully understand the impact of their behavior, but talking can help you sort through the pent-up feelings of pain and resentment.

3. *Be positive:* In order to overcome a serious lapse in judgment or a betrayal, both parties have to make a commitment to stay positive. Try to see your spouse in another, more positive light. Thinking of

some of the nice things they have done in the past will help both of you move past the negative situation.

4. *Be prepared for relapses:* Don't use your partner's relapses as confirmation of their inherent worthlessness. Try to use these times to review your common goals and to strengthen his or her objectives. Depending on how you handle them, relapses can actually help your partner work toward becoming a better person.

Warning Sign #5: Total Avoidance

In my opinion, a lawyer who shies away from a good fight is not a real lawyer. From day one in law school, we are taught to be aggressive, inquisitive, and argumentative. We're often not in the business of making friends, and will always try to get the upper hand in any situation.

That's why in my own marriage, I've been forced to alter my approach to conflict. I have learned to pick my battles at home, and only fight for those things I truly believe in. But while people such as myself may need to curb their aggressiveness on the home front, others need to toughen up and learn to ask more from their significant others.

Greg, a 40-something human resources supervisor, came to see me about separating from his wife Jenna, but I could tell right away that my office was the last place he wanted to be. And the longer he talked, the more I became convinced that his marriage was not something he was willing to abandon without a fight. Unfortunately, the fight had gone out of him.

"When Jenna was offered an incredible job in San Francisco to work as a new media manager, I knew she couldn't pass it up. It meant more money and more perks. She was worried about telling me, thinking I would refuse to relocate, but after getting over the shock, I decided that I was glad to be moving. I had grown tired of the pace in New York and was getting a little fried at my old job. The opportunity came at the best possible time and three months later we were heading to San Francisco. Luckily, I managed to find a job in HR out there. It was as high-profile as my old position, and the more relaxed pace was just what I was looking for.

"We had a great time in San Francisco. The move seemed to bring new life to our marriage. Jenna was in higher spirits and liked her job. Three years later, however, it was a different story. The company she had been working for was in trouble, and she was one of the many to be laid off when they were acquired by a major media conglomerate. To make matters worse, we had just bought a house, and were deciding how to manage our lives from a financial standpoint. Fortunately, my old company in New York was looking for an HR director, and they called me to see if I was interested. At this point, I honestly believed that it would make more sense to move back to New York.

"That's when things really got difficult. Jenna was appalled that I would even make such a suggestion, and told me that I should go back by myself. Seeing her overreaction, I soon realized just how hurt and angry Jenna must have been at losing her job. I looked at the situation from her point of view, and realized that her pride had been hurt. After all, it was her idea to move out there in the first place, and leaving now would be a sign of defeat in her mind. When I tried to broach the issue and help her sort through some of her feelings, she refused to talk to me. She was depressed about losing her job, and told me that her mind was made up, that I should move back to New York and she would stay in San Francisco. The more I tried to get her to open up, the more she was determined to avoid the subject. She was determined to prove that she could get another job, and I had to move back to New York so we could pay our bills.

"Ever since then our relationship has been strained. She found a job in San Francisco, but it wasn't really what she was looking for. I don't know what to do. We live in separate cities so talking has become even more difficult. I just wish she would face me head-on and talk to me about the problem."

I saw that Greg was in dire straits, and that his attempts at a divorce were simply desperate bids for Jenna's attention. I asked him when was the last time the two of them had gone on vacation. "It could be that a change of scenery and time without work may do the trick. Have you thought of maybe getting two tickets for you and Jenna and seeing how things go? And one more thing, don't pressure her to talk about the job and the move. See how things go and let her take the initiative."

Greg thought about the idea for quite some time, and I saw that he was really listening to what I was saying. He looked relieved and thanked me for my time. He promised to let me know how everything went.

I didn't hear from Greg for quite some time, until a few months later when one of his friends called me at Greg's referral. I asked him about what had happened to Greg, and he was happy to report that Jenna and he were living happily together—in New York City.

There are times in every marriage when it's hard enough to face ourselves, let alone our spouses. No matter how often our partner tells us that "it's okay" and "things will work out," there are days when you need to work through difficulties on your own. But no matter how challenging a situation may seem, no matter how complicated or how long it takes you to work through it, it is critical that you keep your spouse in the loop. Whether it's simply by thanking him for offering to help or expressing gratitude about her patience and understanding, there are ways to communicate with your spouse even during those times when you'd rather be alone.

Points to Ponder

1. How often have you walked out of the room during a fight? If this is a pattern, make an effort to face your partner during confrontation, even if what you hear makes you uncomfortable.

   _____

2. Has your partner ever expressed frustration with your avoidance tactics? If yes, take a minute to think about how you would feel if the situation was reversed.

   _____

3. Do you often hold back from telling your partner what you really think and feel? If yes, try to think of your spouse as your best friend, and don't worry about criticism or judgment.

Communication: Crimes and Misdemeanors

Crime and Misdemeanor #1: Arguing for Argument's Sake

Arguing to prove a point is fine when you have millions of dollars riding on the outcome, but when it comes to your marriage, being right isn't everything. In fact, needing to be right can amount to absolutely nothing, leaving you without the affection, respect, and trust of your spouse.

Three years ago I had the chance to represent Susan, a well-known editor-in-chief of a prestigious magazine. She was usually very closed off, but on this particular occasion, I found her to be in a very talkative mood. She admitted to me that she and her husband argued incessantly—so often, in fact, that she couldn't even remember a time when there was peace and quiet in the house. When I probed as to the source of the marital acrimony, she considered the question for a moment, and then, in a moment of insight and clarity, responded "Because I care more about being right than about him."

Judging by the look on her face, it seemed to be the first time Susan was able to be so honest with herself. She finally realized that always being right was the surest way to end up alone.

Points to Ponder

1. Do you enjoy playing devil's advocate? Yes ____ No ____
    If yes, how do you think your partner feels when you
    disagree just for the sake of disagreeing?

    _____

2. Has your partner ever expressed frustration with your
    desire to argue? Yes ____ No ____
    If yes, what can you do to curb being argumentative?

    _____

3. Have you ever started a fight out of boredom?
    Yes ____ No ____
    If yes, can you make an effort to schedule plans that both
    you and your spouse will enjoy?

    _____

Crime and Misdemeanor #2: Turning a Deaf Ear

Most of us aren't born with good listening skills. The ability to listen is
something that must be cultivated. Unfortunately, most people are so
wrapped up in hearing themselves speak, exercising their vocabulary,
and honing their manner of speech that they often forget how golden
silence is, and how it is just as critical to establishing good communication as words are.

When it comes to achieving true intimacy, clarity of self-expression
just isn't enough. Once in a while, it's important to shut up, forget about
yourself, and really focus on what your partner is telling you. I can't tell

you how many times I've heard a couple arguing during a deposition. One time, my client was arguing with his wife about their in-laws. He was trying to tell her that it wasn't in their children's best interests to spend a lot of time with her parents, due to the fact that the in-laws were often going off at a moment's notice and not paying as much attention to the children as he would have liked.

She immediately became indignant, and did everything short of pulling a rabbit out of her hat to account for her parents' alleged irresponsibility. Essentially, both parties were saying the same thing: They were expressing the idea that their children's welfare was their top priority. Had my client stopped to think for a moment, he would surely have realized what I and everybody else in that conference room could plainly see: that his wife was not at all intent on keeping the children with their grandparents; she was merely trying to save face in front of a group of strangers.

Watching them, I couldn't help but wonder how different their lives would have been had they only stopped talking long enough to really listen.

Points to Ponder

1. Do you and/or your partner frequently interrupt each other during arguments? Yes _____ No _____
   If yes, take turns talking. Then repeat what your partner has said after he or she is finished speaking.

   _____

2. Have you ever become so angry that you were unable to listen to what your partner was saying? Yes _____ No _____
   If yes, try taking a deep breath and focusing on what your spouse is really trying to tell you.

   _____

3. Have you ever stopped to think about what your partner is feeling during a confrontation? Yes _____ No _____
   If you focus on your partner's feelings you will be less likely to lose control and will have a better understanding of his or her point of view.

Crime and Misdemeanor #3: Losing Control

At some point in our adult lives, all of us have lost control of our emotions. Frustrations mount, heart rates rise, pulses quicken, and before you know it, you're screaming at your partner for no reason, or at least none that you can remember. Although shouting and raising your voice can have detrimental effects on a marriage, not being able to manage your anger is usually the surest way to effect a total breakdown in the channels of communication.

Stella, a 38-year-old CPA, was on the brink of filing for divorce. We talked about some of her marital problems, and why she was looking to get a divorce after sixteen years of marriage to her husband, Ron, a theater manager.

"When I met Ron," she told me, "I was only 22. I had just graduated college and moved to the city. We met during a post-show party at a small theater, and I was in love instantly. He was everything I was looking for: smart, charming, intelligent, and cultured. Since I was new to the city, he showed me around and really helped me develop as a person. We went to museums, great restaurants, and galleries. A year later, we had moved in together. That's when I realized that Ron had quite a temper. Before we lived together, he was the kindest, gentlest man, but eventually his reserve melted and his true colors came out. He would yell at me during fights, and sometimes he would take my keys so I couldn't leave the house. Of course, we would make up soon after that, and his anger wouldn't last more then a few hours, but I was always on my toes wondering when he would get angry again.

"His attitude and anger really began affecting me, in that I found that I did not want to tell him anything anymore, for fear of getting him mad. I started hiding little things from him. If I went out with a friend he didn't like or bought something expensive, I wouldn't tell him. I figured that the less we talked, the less likely he was to get angry with me. It got to the point that we stopped communicating altogether. We grew further and further apart with each passing day. It's not that I didn't want Ron in my life, I was just scared to let him in."

In the end, Stella and Ron decided to stay together and work on their problems with the help of a marriage counselor. Ron also sought anger-management training, and, from what I heard, improved his communication skills considerably in the process. We've all said and done things in the heat of the moment that we've later regretted. But losing your temper repeatedly can irrevocably alter your marriage to the point where no amount of counseling and communication will be able to bring it back to life. Fortunately, Stella and Ron were able to salvage their marriage in time.

Exercise: Relationship Bill of Rights

We are all entitled to a caring and considerate partner. Answer the following questions about your partner. If the majority of your answers are "no," your spouse may not be meeting your needs. You'll need to open up the lines of communication if you want to have a successful marriage.

1. Is your partner willing to compromise? Yes _____ No _____

    _____

2. Does she or he make you feel comfortable being yourself?
    Yes _____ No _____

    _____

3. Is your spouse able to admit to being wrong? Yes _____ No _____

    _____

4. Does your partner resolve conflict by talking honestly?
    Yes _____ No _____

    _____

5. Does he or she make you feel safe and secure? Yes _____ No _____

    _____

6. Does your partner respect your feelings, even when they differ with
    his or her own? Yes _____ No _____

    _____

Crime and Misdemeanor #4: Emotional Blackmail

Forever is a long time. But when it comes right down to it, we all want to believe that we will be with our spouse for the rest of our lives. That's why we get married to begin with, in the hopes that one day we will enjoy our twilight years with someone who knows us better than we know ourselves.

Security is one of the most important elements of any relationship. Partners who feel that they will always be together are much more open and honest about their feelings. Other couples—those who aren't as certain of their partner's affections—will tend to mask their true feelings, fearing that their words or behaviors will decrease their spouse's affection.

Although a certain amount of mystery can create sparks and add excitement to a relationship, people who consistently strive to keep their spouses in doubt of their feelings are doing their marriage a disservice.

Charlie, a client of mine from ten years back, told me an interesting story. It seemed that every time he fought with his wife, Diane, she would always end the dispute with a threat to leave him. In the beginning of their marriage, Diane's approach served its purpose: Charlie would quickly drop the matter, and let Diane believe that she was in the right. Seeing that her tactics worked, Diane used them more often. She would either threaten to walk out or to ensure that he never saw either of his two children again. Both options scared Charlie to death, and he would always give in during their arguments.

Eventually, Charlie grew to hate Diane. Instead of being a source of comfort and joy to him, she had become an adversary. "I couldn't believe what had become of my wife. Of course, she always had her personality flaws, but I never imagined it would escalate to this extent."

After years of being blackmailed by his own wife, Charlie decided that he could no longer live in fear. He decided to call her bluff, and see what she would do. The last time they fought, Charlie told her to pack her bags and leave the house. Of course, never having any intention of leaving, Diane was flabbergasted by his response. She tried to make amends, but it was too late. Charlie realized that fear, not love, had kept him by her side. Once that realization dawned, he couldn't wait to get out of the marriage.

Points to Ponder

1. Has your spouse ever made you feel obligated to do something you preferred not to do? Yes _____ No _____
   If yes, how did that make you feel?

   _____

2. Have you or your spouse ever threatened to expose family secrets during a confrontation? Yes _____ No _____
   If yes, did you confront your spouse and express your feelings?

   _____

3. Do you trust your spouse with your private matters?
   Yes ____ No ____
   If not, why?

_____

Crime and Misdemeanor #5: Living in the Past

We've all done things we're not proud of. Dealing with our blunders is hard enough the first time around, but imagine if we had to spend the rest of our life sitting in a room and listening to all of our past mistakes being broadcast over a loudspeaker. A pretty bleak picture, wouldn't you say?

Unfortunately, many people find themselves trapped in just this type of scenario. Indeed, it's quite likely that either you or your spouse is guilty of visiting this marital plague upon your relationship. You see, it's very easy to focus on the past when it allows us to avoid taking responsibility for the present.

Take, for example, any common argument between a couple: One partner gets backed into a corner, and instead of admitting wrongdoing or apologizing, that partner turns the tables by blaming the spouse for some irrelevant mistake he or she has committed in the past.

A disagreement I overheard during a charity dinner reminded me of this all-too-common problem. The couple behind me had been bickering all night. The wife, a beautiful woman, was chastising her husband for paying special attention to another attractive woman seated at their table. After going back and forth for what seemed like hours, the husband, who was hoping to end the argument, quickly reminded his wife about the time she once had lunch with her ex-boyfriend without telling him.

From what I could discern, the ex-boyfriend was old news. The couple had probably tried to put the incident behind them, until the man brought it up simply to avoid issuing an apology for his behavior.

Old wounds die hard. The husband had probably been very upset about his wife's visit with her ex. Whether or not he ever got over it, however, is not as important as the fact that instead of dealing with the matter at hand and engaging in open communication, he used his wife's past transgression as a convenient foil to put a quick end to the argument. No resolution was achieved, and no satisfaction derived. If anything, both husband and wife will probably feel slighted, but powerless to improve the situation.

Communication: Effecting a Reconciliation

Reconciliation #1: Prepare a Statement

Nothing is more important to a lawyer than getting all of the facts down on paper. The same could be said for couples. Just knowing what you want to say doesn't cut it. During conversations, most people tend to hear only what they want to hear. Frequent interruptions have a tendency to derail our train of thought. By the time you are able to get your point across, you are often so frustrated with your spouse that you lose the motivation to communicate.

The next time you find yourself looking to get something off your chest or seeking to confront your spouse, write all of your thoughts, problems, and complaints down on paper beforehand. Don't hold anything back. This process will allow you to organize your thoughts in a way that should clear up any confusion and minimize the risk of miscommunication. You may also prevent your feelings from steering your argument off course, a key component of getting a fair hearing for a legitimate complaint.

Once you've completed the letter, look it over. Does it convey all of your feelings? What kind of tone is the letter written in? Does it reflect anger or a determination to work things out?

Having reviewed your letter, you must now decide whether you want to give the document to your spouse or use it as a guide during a face-to-face conversation. If the matter you wish to discuss is especially sensitive and you fear losing control during your meeting, then by all means let the letter do the talking. But if you believe that you will be able to maintain a level head, bring the note with you, and only refer to it when you find the discussion taking a wrong turn.

Exercise: Writing a Statement

Addressing the following issues will help you compose a clear and rational statement.

1. Briefly describe the topic you wish to address.

    _____

2. Have you ever discussed this issue before? Yes _____ No _____
    If yes, what was your spouse's reaction?

    _____

3. List three things you hope to accomplish during the discussion.

    1. _____

    2. _____

    3. _____

4. What are some objections that your spouse might make?

    _____

5. What are some rebuttals that will help you deal with those objections?

    _____

Reconciliation #2: Connect Versus React

As times goes on, some couples forget that their desire to connect with one another is the one thing keeping their marriage together. When we're dating, understanding one another is usually our top priority. But as we grow comfortable with our spouses, we tend to forget that the whole point of getting married was to establish an even stronger bond, to become a strong and functioning family unit.

Couples get so used to defending both positions during conflict that they completely lose sight of this fact: *Every argument is an opportunity for greater intimacy.* Whether you're bickering about finances or in-laws, there is always a way to find common ground. The problem is that each party is usually too wrapped up in his or her side of the debate to remember that they're both on the same side.

No matter what you and your spouse are quarreling about, you must never forget the main objective: *to be heard and understood.* All of us want to believe that our feelings matter to our partner, that understanding who we are and supporting us in our endeavors is one of our partner's top priorities. That is how we measure the success of our marriage. Our conflicts are just so many attempts to prove that our marriages are working out.

So when our partners get on the defensive and refuse to hear our side, we begin to suspect that we have somehow made the wrong decision—that the person we married is not in fact our friend, much less a soul mate. We begin to question the very foundation of our marriage, and that's never a good thing.

Within every argument lies a golden opportunity to find new common ground and grow stronger as a couple. Yet most couples persist in interpreting conflict as a flaw in the marriage, instead of a means of facilitating bonding. Next time you're in the middle of a marital spat, try to connect with something in your spouse's argument, rather than find more things you can disprove.

Once you find the connection, the differences won't seem nearly as important.

Reconciliation #3: Time It Right

As a matrimonial lawyer, I know the importance of being at the right place at the right time. Say the judge has just gotten back from a long lunch and is a little tired, a little lethargic, and in no mood to sort through complicated evidence. So whenever I intend to introduce new material into a case, I try not to do it right after lunch. Mornings are a much better time to get my point across. Everyone's wired off their morning coffee, and brimming with energy and anticipation.

When you communicate your ideas is just as important as how you get your message across. If, for instance, you know your spouse is not a morning person, then by all means postpone conversations about important matters until later in the day. It's not only a matter of common sense; it's a matter of courtesy. By showing your mate that you are being considerate of his or her feelings, any point you make will be met with a much more sympathetic ear.

J.B., a CEO of a major Fortune 500 company, was always on the run. He had the kind of schedule that ran on a minute-by-minute basis. Understandably, he and his wife never had enough time to communicate, always arguing on the run. That eventually ruined the marriage, and he sought me out to handle his divorce.

Soon after, J.B. remarried. Although his second wife, Bea, was not as successful as he was, she also had a high-paying, high-powered job as a senior vice president at a major bank.

J.B. vowed that he would not make the same mistakes again. Dreadfully worried about the prospect of another divorce, he learned a thing or two about communication. When I bumped into him over lunch two years later, I asked him how things were going. Apparently, his marriage was still going as smoothly as it had been the day he first exchanged vows.

Always willing to learn something new, I inquired as to what had made the difference this time around: While J.B. could never even make any time for his first wife, his second wife had expressed a preference for talking things over during a long dinner. Of course, during his first marriage J.B. was never even home for dinner. Now, not only did he make sure that he was home for this special time, but he even made the effort to *prepare* dinner for his wife's arrival! Whenever any issues crop up, both J.B. and Bea were always ready and willing to talk about the small problems before they became huge obstacles. I have every confidence in the success of their marriage.

Exercise: Passing the Baton

1. Arrange for a specific time to meet with your spouse—and the "baton." Make certain that the time is convenient for both you and your partner.

2. Find a talking baton that can be easily held in one hand. As long as one person is holding the baton, the other person cannot speak. The person with the baton has the floor.

3. Once you've made your point, pass the baton to your spouse and ask your spouse to repeat back what you've said. Your spouse cannot begin to make his or her own point until you are satisfied that your message has been understood.

4. Continue to pass and hold the stick, until both of you feel that you have made your respective points.

5. Resist the urge to use the baton to hit each other.

Reconciliation #4: Prioritize Your Problems

You would never see a lawyer enter a courtroom and try to represent two different clients during the same trial—and with good reason. Besides not being able to serve either client to the best of his or her ability, the lawyer would only succeed in confusing the issues.

During one meeting with Jane, a fashion designer, I found out just how important it is to prioritize the issues affecting our lives. Jane and Anthony had been deliriously happy for years. Together, they had started a thriving clothing line, which was sold in the best department stores all over the country. Recently, they had even decided to expand by opening up several boutiques in the New York area. With their faces plastered all over the lifestyles sections of magazines and newspapers, they seemed like the pair who had it all: a thriving business and a happy relationship.

Eventually, this idyllic picture began to fade. Being business partners had initially served to strengthen their marriage, but in the few years preceding their decision to get a divorce, the business had become their foremost bone of contention. Or so they thought.

"We *always* argued about the business, except in the past, we would resolve everything quickly," explained Jane. "But everything changed after the baby. Now, not only were we trying to work out the kinks in our business; we were both equally obsessed with the idea of raising a perfectly happy and confident child. It was like running two businesses simultaneously."

The problem was that every time Jane brought up a concern with the child, Anthony would steer the conversation to their business. When Jane wanted to talk business, however, Anthony was fixated on child rearing. It seemed that the couple was never on the same page at the same time. Frazzled and unable to prioritize their discussions, the couple became more and more frustrated with each passing day. In the end, Jane and Anthony decided to stay together after reshuffling their schedules and setting strict guidelines about what they could and couldn't talk about. It took finding a competent nanny, learning how to keep their business separate from their marriage, and going out on many "dates" to finally rekindle the spark that brought them together in the first place.

Of course, being married and in business together is by no means an easy feat. There are so many issues that often need to be addressed at the same time. But you don't have to own a business with your mate in order to understand just how important issue prioritization is. With so many of life's responsibilities always flitting about our psyches, it's easy to lose our focus. Whether it's our children, our finances, or our work life, there are a million topics that need addressing at any given moment. Rather than hurrying on to the next matter of business before even solving the first, you and your spouse should always remember: Put out one fire at a time. Not only will it save your time and energy, it can also save your marriage.

Exercise: Sticking to the Point

Focusing on one problem at a time can be very difficult, especially when there are so many different issues battling for our attention at any given moment. Following these steps will help you deal with one hot button at a time so you can find a resolution faster.

1. Make a list of topics in order of priority before sitting down for a discussion.

2. Do not progress to the next topic until you have found a tentative solution.

3. If you run out of time, make a note of where you left off and agree to continue from there at the next meeting.

4. If you find your spouse switching gears, gently remind him or her of the topic at hand so you can steer the conversation back in that direction.

Reconciliation #5: What Didn't You Say?

Sometimes it's not what we say so much as what we didn't say that creates the problems in our marriage. Most of us know the "right" thing to say in any situation, but we get so caught up in our own lives that we don't bother treating our spouses with the same tact and civility that we extend to our friends, clients, coworkers, and grocery store clerks.

Sara was a successful interior designer in the Manhattan area. She was known for her impeccable taste and style, and was one of the most sought-after designers in the area. Her husband, Robert, was a human resources executive. And although they loved each other, they had always experienced their fair share of marital strife.

"It all started when I began decorating our two-bedroom condo on the Upper West Side. Robert was considerate enough to leave all the decision-making to me. But no matter how hard I worked to beautify the family home, he never even thought to compliment me on a job well done. Well, for years I tried to convince myself that my husband just didn't share my taste. But I couldn't ignore the fact that he always had a kind word for anyone but me. He was known for his superior diplomacy skills at work, and I resented the fact that he had never once commented on my design skills."

Four years into the marriage, Sara decided to redecorate the master bedroom. As usual, Robert would walk in to inspect the quarters, staring blankly at the space as if he was in a trance. A month passed and Sara was still unable to get a reaction out of her husband. It wasn't until she was hanging up the last piece of artwork that she was finally struck by the extent of her anger. At that point, Sara proceeded to pack Robert's suitcase and book him a room at a hotel. She had had enough of his silent treatment and would rather he ignore the interiors of his hotel room than the bedroom that she had worked so hard to decorate.

The moral of the story is that besides worrying about what you shouldn't say, you might want to pay special attention to what else you should be saying. And if you're ever at a loss as to what that should be, try something that always works: "I love you."

Communication: Closing Argument

Communication skills and styles develop and change with our own personal development. It is important to remember that even though you're communicating well right now, the situation can change dramatically when you least expect it. Any changes—a new job, a new baby, or even a relocation—can affect your ability to communicate with one another. The most important thing is to constantly look out for the warning signs, even if you think your communication needs no improvement.

Sound communication skills depend on a couple's level of security and trust in one another. If you've ever committed any of the marital crimes and misdemeanors of communication outlined, consider that you may be corroding the foundation of your communication network.

Because most of us tend to hear only what we want to hear, you should never underestimate the importance of closing your mouth, putting aside your feelings, and really listening to what your partner has to say.

And remember: Within every argument lies a golden opportunity to find new common ground and grow stronger as a couple.

SEXUAL COMPATIBILITY

What could a divorce lawyer possibly know about sex? More than you can imagine. When clients come into my office, they always begin the conversation by talking about their feelings and emotions, but a half hour into the meeting, the conversation will almost always have turned to sex. Chances are, the client's sex life is not as good as it once was. In fact, I can't recall anybody ever telling me that they wanted a divorce even though their sex life was going great.

The connection and intimacy that a good sex life affords plays a critical role in the well-being of any marriage. In the early stages of relationships, couples sometimes have a harder time expressing their feelings, and often use sex to communicate positive emotions. There are some things that words alone cannot express, and sex allows us to fill in those gaps of communication. As we develop more clear lines of communication with our partners, there is a tendency to rely on sex less and less as a means of communication, which often translates into a decrease in sexual intimacy.

However, even though sexual activity may become less important as a means of self-expression, sexual desire continues to play a critical role in our lives. The catch is that in most cases, it is very difficult for couples to synchronize their desire for sex. One always seems to want it more or less than the other—and that's where the trouble begins.

Couples have a myriad of reasons other than desire and communication for having or withholding sex. Each couple's sex life is as unique as their relationship. Although our sex lives, like our relationships, may not always be as satisfying as they were in the early stages of romance, they can be improved significantly if both partners are committed to making a change. Some couples even say that their sexual relations only get better with the years.

During my fifth year in matrimonial law, I had the pleasure of representing Richard, a dynamic and powerful author. Richard's career had been punctuated by one success after another. He had the patient air of someone who is used to enduring hour-long book signings with dozens of adoring fans hanging on his every word. With major books to his name and appearances on almost every national talk show, it seemed that he had it all, until he ended up in my office, telling me about the friendship that had opened his eyes to the problems in his marriage.

It began when he was looking for a new assistant to help him with his daily obligations like writing speeches and transcribing his manuscripts. When Joshua, a recent Yale graduate, applied for the job, the two men took an instant liking to one another, and eventually became more like friends than business associates. Due to the wide gap in their ages, their conversations usually revolved around two things: Joshua's active dating life and the publishing industry. Having been married for about seven years, Richard often complained about the lack of passion in his marriage. It seems that he and his wife only had sex about once a month, even though Rich's libido required a greater frequency of sexual encounters.

Rich tried to live vicariously through Joshua's sexual experiences. Whenever the young man had a date or a steady girlfriend, Richard would grill him on all the details. Eventually, all this talk about Joshua's sexual episodes made Richard even more dissatisfied with his own sex life. His wife never made an effort at varying their sexual encounters, and would scold him whenever he tried to be creative in bed.

A few years later, Richard came to my office, desperate for a solution to his marital problems. When I asked Rich if Joshua's exploits had anything to do with the problems in his marriage, he responded with an unequivocal "Yes." Joshua's passionate love life only served to reinforce Richard's growing discontent, but he was adamant about the fact that had he not met Joshua, he would still have ended up in the same situation. That's when he told me something I will never forget: He told me that if a married couple put a nickel into a bowl for every time they had sex during the first year of their marriage, they would end up with as many nickels as they would accumulate during the rest of their lives.

At first, I laughed at the notion, thinking Rich was just trying to be witty. But many years of matrimonial law later, I could no longer deny the validity of his theory. One of the most common concerns that my clients brought to the table was a deep-seated dissatisfaction with their sex lives. Whether the sex was too infrequent or too predictable, very few married couples could honestly say that they enjoyed a healthy and passionate love life.

That's when I began asking myself: Was an inadequate sex life part of the marriage bargain? Do we have to resign ourselves to dwindling sex drives and absentee libidos? Isn't there some way to establish sexual compatibility and keep the passion in our marriages?

Once I began my inquiries, I started spotting certain patterns that can lead couples down the path of decreased desire. Through my conversations with clients, I realized that there is a definite set of behaviors that indicate the onset of a sexual valley—behaviors that must be addressed and dealt with if a married couple is to sustain the excitement and arousal levels needed for a healthy and fulfilling sex life.

After I heard Richard's story and the effect his young friend had on his marriage, I knew that all was not lost. I recommended that he try talking with his wife in an honest and nonaccusatory way, and, most important, I suggested he stop using Joshua as a barometer for his own sex life. I also suggested that they seek out the help of a qualified therapist. But before Rich left, I explained that only he could decide what was most important to him. I told him that he should reconcile himself to the idea that their sexual problems might never be resolved, but I also reminded him that the problem would not just disappear overnight. He would have to commit himself to improving the situation, and eliminate any distractions or unrealistic expectations.

Fortunately, I never heard from Richard again. And despite not knowing whether he and his wife worked out their problems, I am hopeful that he walked away with a more realistic and mature understanding of how sex can affect a marriage. Here's how you can go about it.

Sexual Compatibility Assessment

Most people talk about sexual compatibility as if it's set in stone: Either you're sexually compatible or you're not. Of course, the issue is much more complicated than that. There are times in our lives when we feel extremely close to our spouse, and other times when the idea of having sex is not very appealing. Having dealt with a large number of clients and heard an even larger number of stories about inadequate sex lives, I can tell you that what can start out as a beautifully compatible relationship can end up being anything but. The key to keeping the passion alive in your marriage is as easy as simply paying attention to the ebb and flow of your sex life. By filling out the following worksheet, you will be one step closer to making your love life a priority.

1. When was the last time you and your partner had sex? Was it satisfying?

_____

2. Who usually initiates sex: you, your spouse, or both equally?

_____

3. Have you ever felt sexually rejected by your spouse? If yes, explain.

_____

4. List four things you enjoy about your sex life.

_____

_____

_____

_____

5. List four things you would change about your sex life.

_____

_____

_____

_____

6. Do you feel you can communicate with your spouse about sex? Explain.

_____

7. Describe your last sexual conversation.

_____

8. Have you and your spouse ever discussed sexual fantasies? Why or why not?

_____

9. How has your sexual relationship changed since you first met?

_____

10. How do you feel your sex life compares to other couples'?

_____

Sexual Compatibility: Warning Signs

Warning Sign #1: A Sudden Change in Libido

Although it may not be a comforting thought, the fact is that not all sex drives are created equal. After talking to hundreds of clients, I have learned that some people can do just fine with once a month, while others wouldn't think of ending the day without a sexual encounter. Many of my clients don't think twice about entrusting me with the most intimate details of their lives—after all, I am their lawyer. And with all my experience, I've yet to find anything resembling a standard for the "normal" sex drive.

Sometimes, a drastic decrease or increase in our level of desire should be construed as abnormal or ominous. Although there will always be some small degree of fluctuation, all sudden and consistent variations in our libidos should send up a red flag.

One day my client Sarah, an executive assistant, told me a story so odd that even I was surprised—and I've heard every tale in the book. "I know I have a very active libido," said Sarah. "All my ex-boyfriends told me so. Scott, however, was never as into sex as I was. I always tried to motivate him to be more aggressive in bed. But he worked endless hours for a major Wall Street brokerage house, and was always either too stressed or too tired to pick up on my not-so-subtle cues. For years I would complain about our predictable love life to girlfriends. But gradually I got tired of always making the first move and reading one sex book after another in the vain hope of heating up our love life."

Scott was the kind of guy who wears English custom made suits and Hermès silk ties to work, the kind of person who always makes sure to have the best table at the newest restaurants. One day, and quite out of the blue, Scott came home and announced that he had been fired from his job as managing director at an investment bank.

When Sarah tried to comfort him, he became very abusive. He demanded that they have sex, and when Sarah tried to fight him off, he became violent and agitated. He was yelling at Sarah for what seemed like hours. "I thought that's what you wanted!" he kept screaming. Five months later, Scott was still at home. He was depressed and unmotivated. The loss of his job affected him deeply. Not only that, but he refused to be intimate with Sarah. Many months went by without the couple even so much as exchanging one kiss.

Sarah couldn't put the ordeal behind her. She tried to coax Scott into therapy, but he wouldn't budge, telling her that her constant complaining was what had finally pushed him over the edge.

Unwilling to break up her marriage at that point, Sarah sought out the aid of a therapist to discuss the state of the marriage. But while she was busy trying to fix their problem, Scott went in search of a divorce lawyer on the grounds that Sarah's incessant complaints about having more sex led him to feel weak and emasculated, which, according to him, resulted in the loss of his job.

Whether or not Sarah had anything to do with the collapse of the marriage, it was clear that Scott had some serious issues to sort through: issues of self-esteem that had nothing to do with Sarah.

I've dealt with numerous cases where a change in libido was a sign of bigger problems to come. Nick, a police officer client of mine, noticed that his wife Lisa didn't want to have sex with him.

"I couldn't understand the sudden change," he told me. "Everything was going well for us. I had just been promoted, and we were even thinking about moving to a bigger house. We used to have sex regularly, at least once a week.

"Not only that, but our sex life was always very exciting. And it wasn't only me initiating the sex. Lisa would sometimes come up with new ideas, and try new things. So I can't tell you how odd it was when she stopped wanting to have sex. I had to become the aggressor, and the more I asked, the more stubborn she became. I tried talking to her about it. She would make excuses like she was tired or not feeling well, so I recommended that she see a doctor, but she just wouldn't even consider it."

He tried to be patient with her, going so far as to recommend that she see a sex therapist. Within a few months, however, he discovered that Lisa's sexual problems weren't all in her head. Involved in an extramarital affair at her workplace, Lisa had been having sex all along—just not with her husband. Devastated as he was by the event, Nick was eventually comforted by the idea that had he not noticed the change in their sex life he might have still been married to an unfaithful spouse.

Couples should understand the importance of noting any changes in their sex drive. When a partner begins to feel substantially more or less aroused, it is important to pay attention to the underlying issues contributing to the change. Most of all, couples should never try to overlook the sexual shifts that are inevitable. Although most of these may not be anything to worry about, it's always best to err on the side of caution and talk about what sexual changes you're going through as you're going through them.

Points to Ponder

1. Have you ever noticed any changes in your partner's libido? What were they?

   _____

2. Did you discuss these changes or simply avoid the topic?

   _____

3. What do you think caused the changes?

   _____

Warning Sign #2: Avoidance of Intimate Situations

Benjamin, a client who is a long-time psychology professor at a major university, brought a problem to my attention when he began complaining about his wife's strange sleeping habits. A serious and pensive man, he had the look of someone who spent too many nights grading term papers.

"If I went to bed late, she would invariably be sleeping like a baby," he relayed. "And not wanting to wake her, I would retire for the night without so much as kissing her good night. After months without sex, I made a concerted effort to go to bed early, in order to catch her before she fell asleep. But suddenly, she was nowhere to be found. When I called her, I found that she was watching a very engrossing movie on TV. A few nights later, I tried this same tactic again only to learn that she was now surfing the Web. It was only when she was sure I was asleep that she finally crept silently into bed next to me."

Benjamin tried everything. One night he pretended to be asleep, snoring quietly as his wife prepared to go to bed. Just as she was tucking herself into the covers, Ben made his move, but things didn't go exactly as he planned. Angry for being caught off guard, his wife's tone of voice turned hostile as she demanded that he leave her alone. Fortunately, Ben and his wife were able to work things out. She had been keeping a very busy schedule, leaving her without enough energy to pursue a healthy sex life. After much deliberation, the couple decided to make more time for each other. Although their sex life never completely rebounded, Ben believes that had he not confronted his wife, they would probably be divorced today.

Angela, a young kindergarten teacher, faced a similar problem when John, her husband of three months, began avoiding her at night. She tried everything—sexy lingerie, full-body massages, scented body lotions, even a candle-lit oyster dinner—but there was nothing she could do to bring him out of his shell. As it turned out, John had feelings of guilt and shame connected to sex. During the courtship, the couple had abstained from sex altogether, planning on making their wedding night special. Angela has just assumed that John's interest in sex was the same as her own. It wasn't long after she found out how repulsed John was by the concept of sex, and how unwilling he was to do anything about it, that she came to me for a divorce.

If you ask a couple to tell you when they first began to lose interest in sex, the vast majority will not even be able to come up with a rough estimate. As I see it, a great sex life is something most people take for granted in the beginning of the relationship. Unfortunately, the decrease in passion is usually so gradual that it's almost impossible for couples to stop it before it happens. No one thinks it will happen to them.

Points to Ponder

1. How often do you and your spouse go to bed at the same time? Do you think this is because of schedule differences or are other factors playing a role?

   _____

2. Does your partner often come up with an excuse to avoid coming to bed, like work, television, computer? Please explain how this avoidance makes you feel.

   _____

3. Have you ever tried to avoid your spouse before bedtime? Please list some of your reasons for doing so.

   _____

Warning Sign #3: Reluctance to Talk About Sex Life

Barbara, a high-powered fashion executive, came into my office one day and nearly broke down in tears. Always well-dressed and perfectly groomed, Barbara never left the house unless she was dressed to the nines. She was the kind of woman who had three walk-in closets but never enough room to store her extensive wardrobe. And her erect carriage and strong bearing left little doubt about her professional success.

Barbara had been toying with the idea of getting a divorce for years, but wasn't sure she could stand the pain of being alone. Barbara had married a much younger man. An aspiring actor, Danny was the kind of guy few women could resist. Always a little disheveled and unkempt,

Danny's idea of dressing up for a night out was putting on a button-down blue shirt and a pair of ill-fitting khakis. When they first met at an Off-Broadway play, she had been attracted by his youth and free spirit, and he by her experience and success. Despite being as opposite as opposite could be, they had married only one month later.

The relationship had its share of problems from the beginning. Danny loved to go out with his friends on the weekends. That was fine with Barbara, but she soon discovered that his friends were not comfortable going out with a woman her age. Unwilling to let her husband's friends cause a rift in their relationship, Barbara would often stay home while her younger husband partied until the break of day.

Of course, having different lifestyles was something Barbara couldn't complain about. In marrying someone more than twenty years her junior, she had expected to make her fair share of compromises. And since she loved him dearly and was afraid of losing him, she avoided doing anything that might displease him.

In recounting her story to me, Barbara later admitted that her initial fascination with Danny was largely due to the fact that he was extremely sexually attracted to her. At first, Danny was the ideal lover. Kind and attentive, he never made her feel as if there was an age gap. Gradually, however, Barbara began noticing a change in his behavior.

"One evening, after returning from one of his ridiculous guys' nights out, he asked me if a friend of his could spend the night," explained Barbara. "I let Danny's friends stay at the house almost every weekend, so there was nothing so very out of the ordinary about this request. Still, something struck me as odd. First, I had never seen the man before. Most of Danny's friends dress very casually, but this man was extremely polished and was wearing an Armani suit. Unlike Danny's friends, this man looked as if he actually worked for a living."

Despite her misgivings, Barbara didn't want to start a fight, and proceeded to fix up the guest bedroom for Danny's new friend. After falling asleep with Danny at her side, she woke up in the middle of the night to find him gone. And it was only when she called for him that he finally ran in the room, looking rather dazed and confused. Even though she never had any reason to question Danny's sexual identity, Barbara suspected that he had been fooling around with their visitor.

"I knew something was wrong. But I couldn't put my finger on it. Finally, I broke down and told one of my friends what had happened. Fortunately, she set me straight. She confirmed my worst suspicions."

Instead of confronting Danny about his bisexuality, Barbara retreated to what I often refer to as a "safe but dangerous place." From that point on, their relationship turned into a purely platonic one. Barbara was scared to probe into Danny's lifestyle for fear of losing him, but by refusing to discuss his sexuality, Barbara ended up doing just that. Danny thought that Barbara had been aware of his bisexuality all along. He believed that he had made his sexual preferences perfectly clear, and could never imagine that that was the source of their problems.

The lack of sex in their lives made Danny feel as if Barbara had suddenly transformed herself from a romantic figure to a mother figure. Instead of splitting up, however, they decided to seek a counselor to help improve the lines of communication. For the first time, Barbara was able to comfortably express her feelings about Danny's sexuality, which ultimately improved their sex lives. And although they still experienced bouts of insecurity and problems discussing their conflicting sexual needs, they became more accepting of one another over time.

Talking about sex is one of the healthiest activities a couple can engage in. Yet most of us still believe that having to discuss our sex lives or schedule time for sex is a sign of trouble in and of itself. Nothing could be further from the truth. After hearing countless cases in which one or both of the partners complained about their poor sex lives, one thing became very clear: Communication is critical to an active sex life. Once you start talking, you'll find that your spouse probably shares your feelings.

The greatest threat to your sex life is the inability to discuss it openly and honestly. Voicing your sexual needs and concerns is the best way to get the maximum satisfaction out of your marriage, and anyone who tells you different is obviously not comfortable with their own longings and desires.

Points to Ponder

1. How often do you and your spouse talk about your sex life? Are you satisfied with the frequency of these discussions?

   _____

2. Are you comfortable discussing sexual preferences?

   _____

3. Has your spouse ever ignored your efforts to talk about sex? How did that make you feel?

   _____

4. Do you wish you could be more honest with your spouse? If yes, what is standing in the way of total disclosure?

   _____

Warning Sign #4: Fighting About Sex

Think back to the last time you and your spouse talked about sex. Did tempers flare? Were accusations leveled? If so, pay careful attention to what is making you so angry. Are your feelings being hurt because you think that your partner either doesn't love you or doesn't find you attractive? Does a lack of sex make you feel deprived? Does feeling deprived make you feel hostile toward your spouse?

Although you may have good reason to be frustrated and upset with your partner, fighting will actually put more pressure on your spouse to meet your demands. And we all know what it feels like to perform under pressure. Let's just say that performance anxiety is not conducive to great sex.

Frank, an attractive young owner of a thriving Internet venture, was the perfect example of what could happen when a couple repeatedly fights about sex. One of his fantasies included seeing his wife Anne, a professional photographer, dressed up in sexy lingerie, and he would often bring home new additions to her nighttime wardrobe. Anne, on the other hand, hated the idea of getting all dressed up like a sex kitten. She found that wearing the lingerie made her feel embarrassed and even more inhibited. As the years progressed, what had started out as a playful fantasy had turned into a fetish. Frank simply couldn't perform sexually without his wife's role play.

Finally, Anne had enough and told Frank to stop buying her lingerie. Frank couldn't believe his ears. "I thought that women loved getting lingerie," he told me. "Anne's reaction totally floored me. I wish she had told me sooner."

To Frank, buying sexy lingerie was a way of telling his wife that he loved and desired her. He couldn't believe that Anne could make something as "innocent" as lingerie seem so "seedy." Anne might as well have called him a pervert outright, for that was how bad he felt. Confusing Anne's refusal of his gifts with a refusal of his amorous overtures, Frank became resentful and angry. He even started questioning his wife's love for him, reasoning that if she truly cared for him she would wear the lingerie.

As you can imagine, all this arguing sapped the sexiness right out of the lingerie and the couple's sex life. A sexy nightgown was no longer just a nightgown; it became the symbol of all that was wrong with Frank and Anne's love life.

Despite the arguments and disagreements, Frank and Anne were still extremely attracted to each other. This became very obvious to me when Frank explained that for all their arguments he had never even considered cheating on his wife. According to him, she would always be the most desirable woman he had ever met. Simply put, he was still in love.

Anne and Frank eventually reconciled after he received help. It is my sincere belief that admitting his strong and lasting attraction to his wife both to me and to himself brought Frank to a realization about his own issues with female sexuality. He was finally able to perform sexually without the aid of sexy lingerie. I am confident that on that day he went home with a greater appreciation for his wife and their relationship.

Sex can be a lot of things: fun, spontaneous, erotic, romantic. But one thing it is not is a subject worth fighting over. Sex should always be an expression of two people's love and passion for one another, not an excuse to criticize your spouse. Although an honest and open discussion can boost your marriage's sex quotient sky high, arguments will only set it back.

Fighting about how much sex you do or don't have is like fighting about how much you love one another. The very act of fighting negates the point. How can you improve your love life if you're locked in a heated battle of wills that has nothing to do with love and everything to do with getting your way?

You must learn other, nonverbal ways of initiating lovemaking. As Eliza Doolittle said to Henry Higgins, "Show me!"

Sexual Compatibility: Crimes and Misdemeanors

Crime and Misdemeanor #1:
Ignoring Your Partner's Needs

Amanda, a soft-spoken English teacher at a private school, explained what it was that made her want to seek out a divorce from her husband of three years. Gregory, a 39-year-old tax attorney working for a large, multinational company, had always been a very good lover. They had never had any problems with their sex life. In fact, the frequency and duration of their lovemaking was a point of pride for the happy couple.

One year into the marriage, Gregory received a promotion from associate to director of the international tax department in the law firm where he had been working for over five years.

The couple was elated by the prospect of even more prestige and, of course, more money. Amanda admits to having been overjoyed by the prospect of more frequent vacations, a new addition to their Hampton weekend retreat, and a new BMW. Having come from a well-to-do family in Stamford, Connecticut, Amanda had never had to struggle. Still, there were times when she worried about having enough money to start a family and leave her job.

When she heard the news, Amanda immediately left her job, with the intention of having a baby. They even celebrated the positive changes in their life by spending a week in London. The couple stayed at the finest suite at Claridge's Hotel and ate at the trendiest restaurants in town. Gregory had four shirts custom made at Turnbull and Assar, and Amanda even picked out an antique brooch at Asprey's.

The trip went by quickly. Gregory and Amanda were in the best of spirits, a jovial mood that was reflected in their passionate lovemaking. They felt as if they were falling in love all over again—except this time, without all of the insecurities and doubts that accompany a new relationship.

Having toasted to a wonderful new chapter of their life, the couple returned to New York a week later. Amanda visited a physician who offered advice about getting pregnant, and Gregory went off to enjoy the fruits of his labors at the firm. But although the future was ripe with possibilities, the reality turned out to be quite different than what the couple expected. Instead of enjoying and feeling confident about his new position, Gregory felt an immense amount of pressure that he had never anticipated. The firm was a relatively small one by New York standards (just over a hundred lawyers), and he had never expected that being in charge of a cadre of tax lawyers would take so much out of him. Although he had often stayed in the office until 7 P.M., he was now coming home well past 10 P.M. He, along with the other lawyers in the firm, had always coveted the executive position. He never thought twice about the extra responsibilities that would come along with it.

The couple's first week at home was difficult. Amanda recalled the experience: "All I could think about was becoming pregnant, and Greg was worried about his new role at the firm. Sex was completely out of the question. I kept hoping that things would change once Greg got into a routine at work. But instead of changing for the better, they changed for the worse. Months after the big promotion, Gregory was still coming home exhausted and too stressed out for anything more than a few minutes of lovemaking. He performed as if he was fulfilling a tiresome responsibility. Then, once he was finished, he would roll over and fall asleep. Let's just say, I was very disappointed."

Still, Amanda ignored her own needs, rationalizing that having a baby was her main priority. After six months of this, Amanda was beginning to feel as if she hardly mattered at all. Between her husband's job and trying to get pregnant, Amanda felt as if her sexual needs were suddenly of no consequence. She had quit her job, failed to get pregnant, and was extremely frustrated. It wasn't long before Amanda became moody and depressed. All Gregory had to do was infuse a little romance back into their sex life, but when he didn't, a morose and dejected Amanda came in to see me.

With all the stresses that we deal with on a daily basis, it's easy to lose sight of what our partner needs. Forgetting to do your share of the housework, coming home late when your spouse cooks a dinner—these are just some of the selfish acts that can, in the long run, cause a breakdown in your marriage and send your spouse to a divorce lawyer. But there's nothing more destructive than losing sight of your partner's sexual needs.

In many of the cases I've seen, one partner usually complains about being neglected. But neglect in and of itself does not cause people to get divorced; it is their inability to communicate their disappointment and hurt feelings that leads to divorce. Especially where sex is concerned, it can be very difficult to express hurt feelings. There is a morass of pride and self-esteem issues that can keep us from letting our partner know we could use a little extra attention. Getting up the courage to ask our spouse for more sexual attention is much like asking our spouse for more love itself. We feel as if we shouldn't even have to ask. And although that may be true in theory, the reality is that such an attitude does nothing to improve the situation and can lead to even bigger problems down the line.

A certain amount of give and take is expected in any relationship. Where sex is concerned, give and take is crucial to the care and upkeep of a satisfying love life. In other words, there is no room for pride or principles. If you find yourself feeling like you need a little extra attention or if you're concerned that you're not getting the amount of consideration you're used to, you must put your pride aside, speak up, and take control of the situation before it takes control of you.

Points to Ponder

1. Have you ever felt that your partner's job or busy lifestyle was having a negative effect on your sex life?

_____

2. Does your partner make an effort to please you in bed? If not, have you alerted your spouse to your needs? If you did, did he or she make an effort to improve?

_____

3. Do you think about fulfilling your spouse's sexual needs? If not, why do you think that is?

_____

Crime and Misdemeanor #2:
Criticizing Your Partner's Appearance

All of us want someone who will love us not only in spite of our flaws, but because of them. Our sex lives actually depend on it, as I recently learned from a conversation with a smart, wonderful, self-confident woman.

"I couldn't believe him." Beatrice, a search consultant for law firms, spoke through her tears. "Everything I ate was suddenly up for debate. Whether I ordered a dessert or ate too much of my meal, he would either say something cruel or just look at me in that terribly disapproving way. It got to the point that I even thought about getting cosmetic surgery, something I had sworn I would never do."

Sadly, Beatrice's story is not an uncommon one. Beatrice was just finishing up her MBA program when she met Ted, a young and ambitious politician. She fell in love with him almost at first sight. According to her, "He just has this powerful and commanding way about him. He swept me off my feet."

Ted had his life planned down to the minute. He wanted to marry someone who was beautiful, intelligent, and charming. As Beatrice would later admit, "He wanted someone who would look good standing next to him at the podium."

Although she didn't know it at the time, being married to a politician would have just as many drawbacks as rewards. At first, Beatrice and Ted enjoyed an active love life. As a devout Catholic, Ted would not engage in premarital sex. But once they consummated their marriage, Beatrice was relieved to find out that they were sexually compatible.

Two years went by without a hitch, but when Ted decided to run for a local elective office, everything changed for the worse. Ted became even more vigilant about his personal life and career. Everything from his ties to his shoes had to be just right. If Beatrice so much as said something off-key during one of the many political events she was "encouraged" to attend, Ted would criticize her for hours later that night. Still, they were enjoying what Beatrice considered a healthy sex life, with only a few minor problems here and there.

When Ted finally won the election, Beatrice hoped that he would loosen up a bit. But if anything, Ted became even more concerned about his public image. Beatrice later admitted to being pressured into having children. After all, how could a politician preach family values if he had no kids of his own?

In the next three years, Beatrice had a boy and a girl. An extremely devoted parent, she decided to leave her search consulting job to be a full-time mother. During the course of her pregnancies and the upheavals in her life, Beatrice wasn't at all surprised to find that she had gained nearly twenty pounds. She tried exercising at home, but the children made staying in shape difficult. Although she would have liked to lose weight, she never really worried much about it, until, that is, Ted began commenting on her weight gain.

Listening to him offer dieting tips and make jokes about her weight to his friends was very painful. Beatrice knew plenty of women whose husbands didn't give them a hard time for having gained weight due to pregnancies. She was so angry with Ted for making her feel unattractive that she retaliated by refusing to have sex with him.

"I figured that if I'm so terribly ugly and unattractive, why would he want to have sex with me?" Beatrice asserted. "Of course, Ted made all the usual advances. But I was suddenly too self-conscious and embarrassed to change in front of him. I was always worried that he would insult my body while we were in the act of lovemaking, and that was something I couldn't stand. Besides, not having sex with him was the only way I could get back at him for all those hurtful comments. It was my way of saying I wasn't going to take the abuse anymore."

Beatrice considered all her options; she starved herself, worked out with a trainer, and even had a brief consultation with a renowned plastic surgeon. In the end, she decided to file for divorce. For her, it had become not so much a question of saving her marriage, but of saving what was left of her self-esteem.

That's not to say that only women are prone to moments of physical self-doubt and insecurity. There are just as many men who feel as if their wives are no longer attracted to them and spend hours trying to recapture their youthful builds at the local sports club. Sex is very closely tied to our self-esteem. We tend to derive great satisfaction from the knowledge that our partner finds us sexually attractive.

The reason I bring this up is to stress the importance of being sensitive to your partner's feelings. Unfortunately, although a lucky few individuals age with grace and dignity, it's not often that the general populace is blessed by the aging gods. In fact, many of us must rely on our spouses, who remember our glory days, to carry the image of our young and vibrant selves close to their hearts. And whenever we need to shield ourselves from the reality of the aging process, we need only see ourselves through the eyes of our spouses. If anyone can boost an ego, it's a loving partner who can look you in the eye and say, "You haven't changed a bit."

Points to Ponder

1. Have you ever criticized your partner's appearance? If yes, how did you express your dissatisfaction?

   _____

2. Has your partner ever criticized your appearance? If yes, how did you react to the negative comments?

   _____

3. Have you ever tried to improve your appearance for your spouse? If yes, how did your partner respond to your attempts at self-improvement?

   _____

Exercise: Coping with Criticism

Criticism always comes as a bitter pill, whether it's doled out by a well-meaning friend or an unhappy judge. But it can be especially hard to swallow when it's coming from your spouse, someone who should love you unconditionally. There are two common reactions to criticism: people either internalize the negative message or assume a false bravado and lash out at the critic. Still, there are other alternatives that can put a stop to the behavior.

1. *Let them see you sweat*: Pride can help you feel strong and invincible for a little while, but it will do nothing to stop your partner's complaints. In fact, acting like you don't care can actually make your partner even more determined to get a reaction out of you. By showing your spouse that your feelings are hurt, you can begin an honest exchange that may result in more sensitivity on your spouse's part.

2. *Turnaround is* not *fair play*: Holding your tongue when someone else is criticizing you is about the most difficult thing to do, but it is also the most important. By not lowering yourself to your partner's level, all of the attention will be focused on their negative behavior and not yours. If there is any ambivalence as to who's the "bad guy" in the scenario, the behavior will continue.

3. *Don't be a punching bag*: No one deserves to be verbally abused and harshly criticized. So if you find yourself in that situation, simply take yourself out of it. After years spent in litigation, I've noticed that the best thing a witness can do while being interrogated is to remove him- or herself from the situation by drinking water or taking a moment to clear his or her throat. The same goes for you. By leaving the room or taking a brief walk around the block, you will be showing your spouse that they've crossed the line and that you will not tolerate their behavior.

Crime and Misdemeanor #3: Hiding Sexual Dysfunction

Sexual dysfunction usually has a very disruptive effect on a marriage. Any couple experiencing sexual tension or difficulties should make every attempt to rule out the chance of a physical problem before tackling the issue. Most of my male clients who've struggled with impotence complain of having to deal with the embarrassment of telling their spouses, but I can tell you one thing: No amount of embarrassment can ever come close to the emotional strain that goes hand in hand with divorce.

Janice was the kind of woman who always seemed optimistic even in the face of great challenges. Despite the fact that she was going through a rough period in her life, she always tried to be pleasant and upbeat. According to Janice, her husband Gerry, a 40-something TV actor, had all the makings of the perfect family man. "He didn't work himself to the point of exhaustion, avoided the whole Hollywood scene, and is a great father to his son. He's a great guy. Everybody loves him. Even the press never had a mean word to say about him. If only he could have confided in me. I don't even think he ever came to grips with it."

The trouble began right after Gerry won his first major television award. The couple was thrilled with what they thought was an overdue recognition, and were even more excited to usher in the birth of their first child. Having been married for a little over eleven years, Janice and Gerry were comfortable with their sex life, despite the fact that Gerry sometimes wanted to have sex more often than Janice.

So when Gerry became withdrawn and secretive, Janice had no other choice but to wonder if he was cheating on her. "All of my girlfriends with husbands in the industry would constantly taunt me. 'Wait till it happens to you,' they warned. I used to laugh at them. I thought they were just jealous. But suddenly, I had my own reason to worry."

Gerry had never used drugs and was a social drinker at best. Lately, however, he had begun to arrive home inebriated and confused. When Janice demanded that he tell her where he'd been, he would scowl and walk away, saying, "You don't understand. Just leave me alone."

It was obvious that something was bothering him. But the more Janice pried and probed, the more sullen and secretive Gerry became. Soon, Gerry was beginning to pick fights with his wife just so he could avoid sleeping with her. What Janice couldn't possibly have known was that her husband was trying to cope with impotence. Although he had experienced occasional problems before, the dysfunction was never quite so serious. Now, Gerry feared that he would never be able to have sex with his wife again. He worried that Janice would leave him for another man, someone who could better satisfy her sexual needs.

Gerry was so distraught by his deteriorating condition that he began drinking heavily. He knew that Janice suspected him of having an affair. But the funny thing was, he preferred to let his wife think that he was cheating on her rather than reveal the extent of his problem. That way at least he knew that his masculinity would never be brought into question.

The marriage was beginning to strain under the weight of Janice's suspicion and Gerry's secrecy. And it was only during the final stages of litigation, when the lawyers were discussing the trial issues, that the truth finally came out. Fortunately, the two were able to reconcile. When Gerry finally admitted to his problem, Janice was not only understanding, but relieved to find out that no other woman had come between them. It was apparent to everyone in the room that they loved each other deeply. And as far as I know, from their joint appearances at awards shows and various celebrity functions, the couple is still happily married today.

This story brings to mind yet another case early in my career. In this instance, Fiona, a 35-year-old fact checker for a literary magazine, developed a physical condition that made having sex very painful. Worried about the prospect of not being able to bear children, she refused to think about the problem or seek medical treatment. Meanwhile, she was unable to have sex with her husband Danny, an auto mechanic, and he began seeking out the company of other women. The ensuing divorce seemed like a mere formality because Fiona and Danny's marriage had really ended when she refused to face her sexual problem.

Whereas most people will be the first to admit that they're suffering from a headache or the common cold, the thought of complaining of a sexual dysfunction is something that only a rare few will do. Whether it's brought on by medication, emotional turmoil, or a physical condition, millions of people experience sexual dysfunction of some kind. And you'd be surprised at exactly how many of them keep their secret tightly guarded, not breathing a word even to their spouses.

Crime and Misdemeanor #4: Recoiling from Spouse

In my years of practicing matrimonial law, I have found that certain behaviors can irrevocably alter the state of our unions. When it comes to sex, one of the most damaging tendencies I have encountered is when a spouse is so averse to having sex with the other spouse that he or she physically recoils every time the partner makes an effort to become intimate.

The idea that a once loving and physically affectionate spouse is repulsed by any physical contact can have detrimental and long-lasting effects on a person. The spouse who has been rejected often goes through a myriad of emotions, including feelings of rejection, shame, and self-doubt.

Larry was a gregarious, 30-something lawyer whom I had met through friends on several occasions. He was referred to me by another associate, and I was soon listening to him pouring out a similar story in my office one day.

"Beth and I always had a strange and somewhat tenuous sexual relationship. We had met in our late twenties, and I soon found out that she had been hurt before. Early on, she revealed to me that she had many sexual partners before me. So I was surprised to find out that she wasn't very sexually engaged during our encounters. I had to really work to get her in the mood, but once we got going, she seemed to be enjoying herself. Even if the sex wasn't perfect, we had many things in common. She worked as a paralegal at my firm and would often help me with difficult cases. The long hours and the time we spent together drew us closer and closer, until one day I couldn't imagine being without her and asked her to marry me.

"The first three years of our marriage went by relatively smoothly. We didn't fight very often, and would have sex maybe three times a month or so. In the fourth year, we began having sex less and less. I soon found out that it was becoming more difficult to persuade her to have sex. She just didn't seem to be interested, at all. It was during these last few months that I noticed something was drastically wrong. One night, before falling asleep, I reached over to give her a hug and a kiss good night. I knew that she was tired and wasn't even thinking about having sex. But when I leaned over to her, she shuddered and turned away from me. I felt completely devastated. I couldn't believe that a simple attempt to kiss her had made her so jumpy and agitated.

"That first night, I chalked Beth's behavior up to nerves and exhaustion. She had been on her feet all day shopping for a Mother's Day gift with no success. I hoped that explained her strange behavior. The next day, I tried to give her a hug, but she had the same reaction. It was as if she was repulsed by the very idea of me touching her.

"I couldn't believe it had come to this: My own wife hated to be touched by me. I felt like a pariah, like I had done something terribly wrong and I began to be ashamed of myself. Soon, I became afraid of touching her at all, fearing that she would have the same negative reaction to me, and I stopped making any attempts at intimacy at all." It took Larry several years to feel good about himself again. He has since remarried, but I always sympathized with what he had gone through.

In a similar case, I represented a man whose wife was divorcing him on the grounds of physical abuse. But what was really interesting was her interpretation of physical abuse, which was her husband asking to have sex with her. Her relationship to sex had become so strained and traumatic that she began to think that something as natural as sexual relations with one's spouse could be considered physical abuse. And it's not as if the couple had never enjoyed a good sex life. She had given birth to six children during the marriage.

Points to Ponder

1. Have you ever felt averse to your partner's touch?
   Yes ____ No ____
   Did you express your feelings?

   _____

2. If you answered "Yes" to the previous question, did you feel guilty about your behavior?

   _____

3. If you've ever recoiled from physical contact with your spouse, what are some contributing factors that may have led to this reaction?

   _____

Sexual Compatibility: Effecting a Reconciliation

Reconciliation #1: Share Your Fantasies

Our likes and dislikes are what make us who we are. Usually, we're only too happy to share our feelings on everything from Thai food to salsa dancing. Yet, when it comes to voicing our sexual turn-ons and turn-offs, we are unable to voice our opinions with the same conviction.

It goes without saying that one person's turn-ons may be another's turn-offs. But the only way to discover what sexual fantasies you and your partner have in common is to talk about them openly.

Leonard, a college basketball coach, lived in a small town just outside of New York City. He was the kind of guy who spent most of his days in sweats, and wouldn't dream of putting on a suit unless he had a game to attend. He had been drawn to pornography ever since he reached puberty. Like any good mother, his would chastise him for looking at his father's *Playboy* magazines. As he grew up, Leonard turned into a very good-looking young man. He was never without an attractive girlfriend. But his interest in pornography did not wane. Many of his girlfriends would uncover his stash of adult movies and magazines, only to rebuke him for looking at what they considered "dirt." Many of them wondered why he needed to look at other women when he could look at them.

Many years and girlfriends later, Leonard developed a complex about pornography. He became vigilant about hiding the contraband, and dreaded being found out. When he finally met his wife, Laura, a professional cheerleader, he fell in love, and vowed that she would never discover what he now considered "his perversion." Although he would still enjoy watching adult movies and looking at magazines, he made sure to limit this behavior to the times when Laura went out of town.

"I usually kept the movies at the bottom of my sock drawer, where no one could find them. One day, when Laura was away, I forgot to eject the tape. The realization hit me at work, but fortunately, Laura wasn't due back for another two days. Still, the tape was all I could think about during that day's practice. When it was over, I rushed home only to walk in on Laura sitting in front of the television, watching one of my movies. I nearly had a heart attack. My face got all red and I couldn't look her in the eye. I kept stammering and looking for a way to get out of there. She told me that it was okay, but I couldn't deal with it. I felt so exposed that it became more difficult to enjoy sex with Laura. I started thinking that she was always judging me."

Within months, the couple was thinking of separating. But even though he seemed to be committed to a divorce, after talking to him I could tell that Leonard needed help and suggested that he see a mental health professional. Two years later, the two were still together. The entire incident of wanting to get a divorce, as it turns out, had been a product of Leonard's misperceptions and his inability to communicate his needs to his only too willing wife. Right now, you and your spouse may be experiencing the same form of miscommunication. You may be keeping something back that may actually improve the quality of your sex life. So instead of hiding your turn-ons under a bushel or, for that matter, in a sock drawer, by all means, share your fantasies with your partner. And don't be surprised if the response you hear sounds a lot like, "What took you so long?"

Points to Ponder

1. What was the most passionate encounter you ever had with your spouse? Describe it.

   _____

2. Has a romantic or sexy movie scene ever aroused you? How did it inspire you to behave?

   _____

Once you've answered the foregoing questions, it is very important that you make a concerted effort to define your fantasies. Armed with a strong understanding of what excites you, you'll have no trouble communicating these findings to your spouse.

Reconciliation #2: Embrace Spontaneity

There are some people who will tell you that the best way to find time for sex is to schedule it into your life. And although that may sound good in theory, I can tell you that it doesn't work for everyone. Some people can't imagine anything less exciting than . . . 8:45 P.M. put kids to bed; 9:00 shower; 9:15 sex.

Blocking out space in your calendar for quality time, like going out to dinner or a movie, makes sense, but scheduling time for love may put too much pressure on the couple to perform. Most people can't predict when they'll be in the mood to have sex. It either happens or it doesn't.

So, the question remains, how do you make sure that you don't feel deprived without taking all of the passion out of your love life? It's a simple matter of taking your opportunities as they arise.

For many of us, sex has become an act laden with ritual. Most people go through too many steps before they are actually ready to have sex. There's the long shower, the occasional massage, the selection of music, and the slipping into something more comfortable. And although all of these elements can make for a very sensual evening, you will probably not have time to incorporate all of them every time. The point is not to get so hung up on the ceremony of it all that you forget that sex can be fun and exciting all on its own. Save the pomp and circumstance for special occasions, but enjoy your sex life on a regular basis.

Not having to go through all these rituals does not mean that you and your spouse love each other less. On the contrary, it means that both of you are sensitive to each other's time constraints, and will do whatever it takes to be together.

Patty, an advice columnist and long-time friend, once told me about how she and her husband would frequently drop everything to have sex. They would sneak off to the bathroom during a boring dinner, have sex in her office during her lunch hour, and enjoy quality time right before running off to work in the morning. And even though they had their share of problems, she would often cite their strong sexual connection as the reason for their enduring marriage. Although I'm not necessarily advocating sex in public places, I know that by trying to be flexible and spontaneous, you will always find a few moments to be with the one you love.

Points to Ponder

1. When was the last time you and your spouse had a spontaneous sexual encounter?

   _____

2. Can you think of any activity—household chores, job— that has kept you from having sex with your spouse in the past?

   _____

3. Does it take you a long time to get in the mood for sex? If yes, please explain.

   _____

4. What are some rituals that you go through before having sex?

   _____

Reconciliation #3: Don't Take It Personally

Daniel and Susanne lived in an imposing house thirty miles outside of the city. Despite being a successful real estate entrepreneur, Daniel was never too busy to indulge his love of sports, including tennis and golf. He even had a large room in the house turned in to his own personal fitness center. Susanne also led a fairly content existence. She had quit her job as a nurse to spend her days taking care of their two kids and shopping with her friends.

Daniel's main complaint was that he felt his wife no longer loved him. I assumed she was having an affair, and was surprised to discover that Daniel's problem wasn't as great as he imagined. At some point, Daniel failed to realize that marriage wasn't the perfect fairy tale of passionate lovemaking followed by a comfortable night in front of the fire. He had gotten married very young, and didn't really understand that his wife's occasional refusal of sex had nothing to do with her feelings for him.

When I asked him how often they had sex, I was even more surprised to find out that it was at least four times a month. Of course, the fact that Daniel wanted to have sex every night made it seem as if Susanne rejected him most of the time. And, as Daniel later admitted, he did have a tendency to ask for sex at the most inopportune times (while she was on the phone or in the middle of finishing her work). It was almost as if he was asking to be rejected. Certainly, Daniel's worries about his wife's lack of interest was understandable. In the first blush of their romance, the two could hardly keep their hands off each other long enough to make it through a family dinner. Her waning sex drive caused Daniel to question their relationship. What if Susanne was no longer sexually attracted to him? The mere possibility came as a great blow to Dan's ego.

When Daniel told me his story and brought up the subjects of sexual incompatibility and sexual abandonment, I quickly suggested that he try turning the tables. I recommended that he change his approach, and instead of always taking the initiative, try waiting for his wife to come to him.

It was Daniel's inexperience that led him to believe Susanne was no longer in love with him. Not having sex every night or being rejected once in a while is normal. Of course, with his small frame of reference, Daniel couldn't possibly have known that. In the end, the couple decided to stay together. The lesson they learned (and it is a lesson that applies to all marriages, not to mention life in general) was to maintain a positive attitude, especially when all evidence points to the contrary. Because if there's one thing I know for certain it is that your sexual relationship won't be perfect all of the time. But if you stay positive about yourself and are sensitive to your partner's needs, the good times will undoubtedly outweigh the bad.

Having your sexual advances rejected is never pleasant. In our single days, it could mean the difference between a healthy self-esteem and spending the night listing all of your flaws. But now that you're married, don't you think it's time you lightened up? You already know your partner loves you. So why does being put off one night still have the power to make us feel as if our egos are out on the line?

It's really a simple matter of not taking everything so personally. There are countless reason why your spouse may not be in the mood for sex: a bad day at work, a fight with a friend, or a physical ailment. It could be one of a million little things that have little or nothing to do with you.

Exercise: Not in the Mood?

Sexual desire is not a switch we can flip on and off at will. Since so many factors contribute to an underachieving sex drive, your first order of business should be to find out what is troubling your spouse. Not only will voicing your concern help your spouse open up about his or her problems, but it will keep you from taking your spouse's rejection personally.

The most common reasons I have found for low sexual desire include:

- stress

- physical discomfort

- exhaustion

Reconciliation #4: Always Remember:
There's No Place Like Home

We all talk about wanting to get away from it all, but if there are any plans that are made to be broken, getting away from it all is the one. Whether it's escaping from your work, friends, in-laws, or even children, the need to leave everything behind and rediscover our partners comes over everyone from time to time. Very few of us, however, ever get around to the task of putting all our worries aside so we can just enjoy being with the one we love. There never seems to be enough time or money to spare, and we end up hoping and praying that somehow, some way, someday our sex life will recharge without any prodding.

You see, most people believe that sex itself is an escape from the everyday. But sooner or later, the quality of our lovemaking begins to mirror the quality of our lives. And if your everyday life is like most people's—full of stress, anxiety, and tedious obligations—your sex life will gradually begin to feel like more of the same.

I had been friends with Glenn and Candice for about six years. When I first met them, they'd just bought their first house together. Through her tenacity and terminal inquisitiveness, Candice had made a name for herself as a first-rate journalist. Glenn, a tall, friendly fellow, was also doing well for himself trading commodities. Somehow our paths kept crossing at various social functions, and we were eventually spending more and more time together. Despite never having gotten to know them as individuals (they always seemed to be two parts of one cohesive whole), I assumed they were both generally content with their relationship.

A time came, however, when I began hearing rumors about their marriage. People were saying, "Oh, did you hear about Glenn and Candice?" "I can't believe they're having problems." Being so busy with my job at the firm, I hadn't heard anything. So when Glenn finally called me for advice, I was more than a little curious. It was an all-too-familiar story: A perfectly happy couple that I thought would stay together indefinitely was considering splitting up.

"I'm at the end of my rope," Glenn told me in my office.

"But you and Candice seemed so happy. Of course, we all have our problems, but how did it come to this?" I inquired.

"It was one thing after another. Yeah, we were happy at first. We were practically inseparable. We got that one-bedroom on Sutton Place, and Candice spent hours decorating it. I was really happy there. Candice was, too, for a while. Then she began to work on her book. The research sent her overseas often. She got to go to some nice places—Paris, London, Japan. I couldn't help wanting to be with her, to get away from it all. We hadn't slept together for something like six months, and I couldn't be away from her any longer. We planned a couple of trips together, but all Candice would do is run around from one source to the next. I hoped that the romance and strangeness of these foreign places would rekindle that spark we had lost. But I don't even think she noticed that anything was missing. Time and again, I'd return to New York feeling as if I had somehow failed. I became convinced that if a romantic place like Paris could not put our sex life back on track, that it was definitely beyond repair. I guess I kind of gave up on everything."

Hearing my friend describe the downward trajectory of his marriage made me sad. But not for the reasons you may think. I was sad because I knew they were giving up prematurely. I wanted to share my feelings with him and told Glenn that there was no "miracle" cure for a fledgling sex life, that Paris, for all its beauty and twinkling lights, could not be relied upon to revive a sexual relationship.

What Glenn was looking for was right at home. Despite Candice's absences, I knew that had he tried to work with the elements that were already in place, the marriage could be saved. I suggested that he make more of an effort to make their home the romantic getaway he thought Paris would have been. I shared some of my findings with him, and was pleased to see that he was listening intently. That alone proved to me that he was not ready for that final step, and I was right. Glenn wanted to make things work very badly, and returned home to his wife with a new resolve.

Sometimes, spending a quiet night at home can be the most romantic and exciting thing you can do. Although many couples go on vacation to breathe new life into their unions, no matter how well the relationship progresses abroad, it will eventually settle back into its old routines unless the problems are truly confronted.

Instead of seeking an escape route at the first sign of trouble, it is important to think about what you have. With a little creativity, you can change old habits that have been sabotaging your love life. Instead of having Chinese take-out for the third straight night, get some long-necked oysters to go. Instead of having sex in your bedroom, move the festivities to the living room carpet. Instead of coming home and watching television, try coming home and giving your spouse a long kiss. He or she might not notice the difference right away, but believe me, your sex life will.

Sexual Compatibility: Closing Argument

Maintaining a healthy and active sex life through the years is a trying and often daunting task. We find that with all our responsibilities and obligations, sex is the first thing to take a backseat. One of the first things that can threaten your sex life is the inability to discuss it openly and honestly. Your sex life will not always be perfect, but discussing it in an open way will insure that you get through the problems as they arise. Certain behaviors and conflicts can make the task even more daunting. If you find that you're guilty of fighting about sex, neglecting your partner, or trying to avoid sex by creating distraction, it is not too late to make amends and bring fun back to the bedroom. Forgiveness can come to even the guiltiest of parties provided they make an effort to change.

Most important, don't worry about whether your sex life is "normal." There isn't one standard for a healthy sex life. Some couples are comfortable with fewer sexual encounters, while others may need to engage in sex on a daily basis. The key is to talk about what's right for you and to do what comes naturally. And although your sex life may not always be what you expected, it can provide a mutual satisfaction and closeness that will keep your marriage together.

MONEY

When a new client comes in to see me, the conversation inevitably turns to money, usually sooner rather than later. Sometimes I think that if it wasn't for money, I would be well near out of business. After all, most of my clients are either trying to increase their assets or protect them from being taken away.

The fact is that whether they be solid as a rock or fragile as china, all marriages have their share of financial struggles. Furthermore, most couples not only confront these monetary issues during their marriage, but they continue to grapple with them long after the union has ended. In the old economy, you got married and settled down. There was no question as to who was going to support the family or who would manage the finances. Today's couples, however, are fortunate enough to have their share of financial conflict prior to getting married. I say fortunate because whether conflict comes in the form of a prenuptial agreement or a shared domicile, there is no better time to assess financial expectations and individual spending habits than when two people are still getting to know each other.

Of course, even a prenuptial agreement is a poor indication of a couple's ability to successfully co-manage their finances down the line. Before the millennium, I had the pleasure of preparing a prenup for Walter, the chief operating officer of a Fortune 500 company, and Jane, a professional image consultant. Having been married once before, Walt knew what it was like to go through a messy divorce. When his first wife, Camilla, discovered that he had a relationship outside the marriage and wanted out, she was so angry and hurt that getting the settlement she believed she was entitled to became a matter of principle.

During the negotiations, Camilla got most of everything she wanted, and then some. As the meeting was coming to an end with almost everything agreed on, the issue of who would get the three family cars surfaced. Camilla immediately demanded that she needed all three. That's when Walter began crumbling. He demanded a moment of privacy with his wife's lawyer, at which point they entered a large, wood-paneled conference room. Once inside, this very buttoned-down CEO calmly climbed on top of the very large antique conference table and began doing something very strange in a slow, methodical manner. He took off his shoes, his socks, his shirt, his glasses, and then finally his pants, until he was wearing nothing but his boxer shorts. Finally, he yelled to his wife's attorney, "If you want the sweat off my back, you can have that, too!"

As evidenced by this unique incident, Walter had been traumatized by the first divorce. He never intended on remarrying, until he met and fell in love with his current fiancée, Jane. She was very understanding about the financial arrangement. Despite the fact that it was her first marriage, she readily agreed to signing the prenup. At that time, it seemed as if she could subsist entirely on love and a boundless optimism. She professed that she couldn't care less about Walter's bank account. After all, she was in love. And although Walter had a decidedly more severe air, he proved, to Jane at least, that he was very much in love himself by the generous allowance he made for his wife in the event of another divorce.

Three years went by and I hadn't heard from the couple. All I knew was that soon after marrying, they'd bought a sprawling property in Scarsdale, New York. But one day, I received a call from Walter. The way he explained it, his wife was going crazy.

"I don't know what to do with her. She's buying up everything. I talked to her about it, but the more I talk, the more nervous she gets. She went to see a therapist, and after a $200 session, he told her she was a compulsive shopper. I could have told her that for free. I mean, you saw her. At first, she was so careful about spending money. Everything was about 'This is your money, I wouldn't dream of spending it.' Now it's become more about 'I wouldn't dream of *not* spending it.'"

Walter had a right to be concerned. Jane had been displaying some pretty abnormal patterns of conspicuous consumption during the past year. But what he didn't tell me until later was that her strange behavior only began when she discovered that Walter had been contemplating another divorce. Although the couple reconciled some of their differences, Jane was obviously still concerned. Worried that he might leave her and take his money with him, Jane's knee-jerk reaction had been to bury her fears and sorrows at Barney's and Bergdorf's.

You see, Walter and Jane shared a complicated relationship, but their relationship with money was even more complex. Jane equated money with security. So when her marriage was threatened, she did what people do in expectation of future deprivation: She stocked up. In the beginning of their marriage, Walter and Jane assumed that a prenup was a simple way to circumvent the question of money. Of course, this was much like putting a Band-Aid on a gunshot wound—no matter how hard you try to avoid it, you'll eventually have to deal with the role money plays in your marriage.

If you're like most people, personal questions concerning money often feel, well, personal. Quick, think about a stranger probing you about how much money you made last year. How much did you pay for your new house? What about that new car? And while you're at it, how much did those new shoes set you back? You see? All of us, no matter how laid-back or grounded, get squeamish when probed about our net worth. Money is an extremely touchy subject. It's a subject no one wants to think or talk about, but one that all of us will inevitably have to address.

For every marriage, money poses a unique set of complications and issues. Every client who comes into my office has a unique relationship with money. Some are born savers, others hoarders, and others still are committed spendthrifts. Some see money as a path to freedom, some to status, some to self-preservation. Just as there are no two people or snowflakes alike, there are no two people whose relationship with money is the same. Now take your average couple. Both enter into the marriage with their own ideas and approaches to money.

You see, there are no rules that people can follow to achieve successful money management. What works for some people would never work for others. In effect, what often ends up happening is that couples fail to grasp the importance of working out their own system, and instead rely on the guidance or, rather, misguidance, of friends and parents to show them the way.

The key to achieving financial harmony is to find a method of money management that works for you, an approach that is tailored to your money management styles as a couple rather than as individuals.

I can think of one couple who illustrates this point perfectly. Hannah and Leonard had been married for twelve years. She was a full-time mom, while he worked as an account executive in a consulting firm. When Hannah came into my office, she broached the subject of money and how it had affected the marriage.

"Lenny has always been tight with money. He never gave me a credit card and put me on a strict allowance since the day we first got married. There were times when I would have to practically beg him in order to buy something special. But I soon got used to it. It became a routine. Whenever I wanted to make a large purchase, I would butter him up for weeks. Anything he wanted. It became a routine, and I was perfectly fine with it. Even when my friends found out our lifestyle and started telling me to leave him, I knew I never would. It may not have worked for them, but it was perfectly fine for me and Lenny."

In the end the couple divorced, but the main issues underlying their divorce had nothing to do with money! Had Lenny stayed faithful to Hannah, she would never have left him. And although some women would balk at the concept of having to "beg" their husband for money, Hannah had accepted her situation, thinking it was normal. I raise this example of Hannah and Leonard to point out that there is no standard way of dealing with money. If it works for you, go with it. On the other hand, if something *doesn't* feel right, even if you're sure that what you're doing is common practice or the right thing to do, address the issues before they turn into problems.

But what about love, you say? Isn't it just as important as money? And what would be the use of money, if we didn't have a loved one to share it with? Well, that's a valid point. The union of love and money is often strained and difficult. Just ask anyone who's ever been in love with someone poor. Or someone who married for the love of money. Are the two mutually exclusive? Are they one and the same? Do two people in love have to deal with the issue of money or avoid the topic like the plague lest it impinge negatively on their romance? After dwelling on the subject for years, I discovered that there were many questions that remained unanswered. It's only now, after years of practicing matrimonial law, that I can honestly say that I have found the answers that will help you reconcile some of the inherent contradictions between love and money.

Money Assessment

Money is a tough issue for the majority of couples I've seen in my office. Even more important, it continues to be a bone of contention for many couples still struggling to stay together. But what is worse than not having enough money is quibbling over money to the point that it causes a rift in your marriage. Take it from me, even people with money to burn can find their marriages adversely affected by the distribution of funds, conflicting money management styles, and an inability to budget soundly. By completing the following assessment, you can pinpoint your weak areas and start learning to cope with monetary issues and concerns.

1. How much time do you and your spouse spend thinking about money?

_____

2. How often do the two of you argue about money? What are some of the issues raised?

_____

3. Do you ever get angry at your spouse for spending too much money? How do you express your anger?

_____

4. Does your spouse ever get angry with you for spending too much money? How does his or her criticism affect you?

_____

5. Do you ever feel like no matter how hard you work to save money, you never seem to have enough? Explain.

_____

6. Do you worry about your retirement and saving enough money for your children's college tuition? Explain.

_____

7. Have you and your partner worked out a practical budget that works for both of you? Explain.

_____

8. Who do you feel is more responsible when it comes to managing money, you or your spouse? Does your partner share this belief?

_____

9. Has the issue of who earns more ever crept into your conversations about money? Does that inequality affect your spending behavior?

_____

10. Have you ever bought a luxury item ($500 or more) without
    consulting your spouse first? How did your spouse react?

_____

11. Have you ever hidden assets from your spouse to protect yourself?
    How?

_____

Money: Warning Signs

Warning Sign #1: Poor Credit

A poor credit history is important to determine in the early stages of a
relationship. It will tell you a lot about a person's attitude and approach
to finances. Melanie, the cofounder of a venture capital firm, was seeking a divorce from her husband David, a public relations executive. In
college, David was always forgetting to pay his bills and owed money to
everyone, including Melanie. She had been aware of his poor money
management skills and poor credit rating at the time, but hoped that he
would get his finances in order during their marriage.

As part of his job, David was always taking clients out for lunch,
dinner, and drinks. According to Melanie, his life was a succession of
meetings that resulted in nothing more than friendly banter. Basically,
when it came to generating new business, David was more a washout
than a rainmaker. Of course, having made so much money of her own,
Melanie always supported David. She wanted him to pursue his goals,
and hoped that he would one day come into his own professionally.

"I had gotten used to managing all of our finances. David didn't
even know how to write a check or pay the bills. And I didn't mind it at
first, until I began receiving phone calls about unpaid tabs at bars and
several bounced checks. I didn't know about it at the time, but it seemed
that David was spending more money than we had agreed on. When I

questioned him about it, he told me that he was looking to take out a loan for a new office space in midtown Manhattan. The last thing he needed was a new office. He had a great set-up in a small space we had found, and his company wasn't even doing as well as it used to. The idea of renting an even more expensive space seemed ridiculous. When I told him how I felt and that I wasn't going to overextend myself financially for something we didn't even need, David started screaming about how I always tried to belittle him and control him."

With the aid of a sophisticated accountant, Melanie tried to help David sort out his financial difficulties. But the more she tried to help and curb his spending, the angrier and more resentful David became. My client endured all of the marital and financial challenges that her husband's money management style created, but it was only when David threatened to transfer all of their joint finances into his own private account that Melanie finally realized that what had started with the issue of a poor credit rating had morphed into something entirely different.

When she came in to see me, Melanie was very frazzled, even scared about what David would do with their money. I realized that David was simply lashing out. He had obviously felt incapable of handling his money on his own, but when Melanie tried stepping in to assist him, he felt even more incompetent and tried to gain control with threats and accusations. Melanie realized that David felt as if he was losing control of his finances, and was trying to get back at her for taking away his autonomy, when in fact she was simply trying to help him get his finances back on track.

Despite his poor attitude and inability to handle his own accounts, David benefited from the aid of a financial manager who helped him isolate the core problems in his money management style. Checking on everything from unpaid bills to bounced checks to defaulting on loans is, in my opinion, fair game. By no means am I telling you to fall out of love at the first sign of a poor credit rating. What I am saying, however, is to become more aware so you can stop poor financial habits before they affect your marriage.

Banks and credit card companies check our credit reports every day.

So what's so wrong with you wanting to be aware of your partner's financial history? If anything, it will reveal a lot about your partner's financial future. Unless your partner is motivated to make a change on his or her own, there will be very little you can do to remedy a lifetime of poor money management. Just as your partner is unlikely to change as a result of your marriage, so is his or her credit rating.

By being aware of David's credit history, Melanie was able to point out problems early on in their relationship before they developed into large, insurmountable difficulties. Still, it was her ability to step aside and let David work out his problems on his own that ultimately saved the marriage. No one enjoys playing a subordinate role in a relationship, especially when it comes to money. Being aware of your partner's credit history is important—but so is ensuring that your partner doesn't feel controlled or manipulated.

Improving Bad Credit

Bad credit does not have to follow you for the rest of your life. There is a solution. Even if you've made mistakes in the past, making a series of concerted efforts to repair your credit will help you and your partner start on the road to a sensible savings plan.

1. Limit yourself to one credit card.

2. Sign up for a debit card.

3. Try to pay with cash whenever possible.

4. Always try to pay more than the minimum monthly payment, since that only covers the finance charge and doesn't lower your balance.

5. Pay on time. If you're so much as one day late, you may be charged as much as $25 to $30 in late fees.

6. Obtain a copy of your credit report from a credit bureau like Experian, Equifax, or Trans Union. You have a right to get it.

Warning Sign #2: Money Micromanagement

The previous scenario emphasized the importance of spotting trouble-some financial situations before they snowball into a full-blown irrec-oncilable difference. Yet there's also something to say against erring too far on the side of caution or trying to micromanage your partner's spending habits.

One of the most difficult adjustments for any couple is learning how to manage their finances as a team as opposed to individually. It is hard enough to figure out how to budget for one, only to have to begin anew, and start budgeting for two. It can take years for someone to get their own finances in order. Then, when a new person is introduced into the equation, many people feel panicky about changing the status quo.

Even when the initial kinks of money management are ironed out, unforeseen factors such as loss of a job or emergency expenditures can wreak havoc on a couple's sense of financial well-being. Oftentimes, one person can react negatively by trying to control a spouse's spending habits and monitoring every little expense from dry cleaning bills to grocery shopping receipts. Whether or not that person has legitimate cause for concern, trying to control your spouse's financial life will inevitably lead them to feel out of control and helpless. When you tell your spouse you know best, irresponsible behavior on their part is bound to follow. It's a self-fulfilling prophecy; if you expect your loved ones to fail, they most likely will. Marriage is a two-way street, and as such it requires that everything, including the household finances, be treated as a team effort.

Warren, a down-on-his-luck entrepreneur, came from the family of an affluent Memphis businessman. Soon after completing business school, Warren moved to New York to "make his mark on the world," as he called it. As the scion of such a successful and prominent family, War-ren always felt that he didn't quite measure up. One of his brothers had a thriving medical practice in his hometown, while the other had opened what had become an important art gallery in London. As the youngest child, Warren always felt as if he had his work cut out for him. And although his parents constantly offered him all the luxuries and connections money could buy, Warren was determined to make it on his own.

Soon after relocating to New York, Warren met Olivia, a struggling actress who lived in a studio on Manhattan's Lower East Side. She was a beautiful young woman with striking dark eyes and wavy blond hair, and Warren found himself in love after only a couple of dates. The two moved in together within a few months of their courtship.

According to Warren, "We never had any money, and that was just fine by me, even when we had no electricity for a couple of weeks. We were so much in love that it didn't matter. But the good times ended shortly after I started my first business, an import/export company that left me in worse financial shape than ever. I had sunk what little savings we had into it. On top of that, Olivia discovered that she was pregnant. I had never been so scared in my entire life. Even though it meant admitting to being a failure, I decided that our living conditions were unsuitable for a growing family. This wasn't just about me anymore. I wanted the best for Olivia and the baby, and decided to move back home with my family. Fortunately, they received us with open arms. My mother even had my old room turned into a nursery for the baby. It was great for a while. I thought we would just stay long enough for me to get my feet back on the ground, but the weeks turned into months and the months into years."

Warren continued living at home with Olivia. But he couldn't shake the sinking feeling that he'd failed his family. He was now thirty-two years old and still living off his parents, borrowing money whenever he could bring himself to ask. To compensate for his parents' boundless generosity, Warren became very strict about his wife's expenses. Every penny she spent reminded Warren of his inadequacy, which, in turn, created even more worries about his wife. He felt out of control and scared. What was stopping his wife from leaving him? Because he wasn't supporting her, Warren felt as if he had no voice in his marriage. So to regain a certain measure of control, he began demanding daily accounts of Olivia's expenses. Everything from the baby's formula to lunch at a fast food restaurant had to be recorded in a big book of expenses. At first, Olivia put up with Warren's behavior. She, too, felt guilty about borrowing his parents' money. But when Olivia suggested finding work for herself, Warren wouldn't hear of it. "I told her that it would disgrace the family, as if I wasn't doing just fine in that area all by myself," he explained.

Unable to pursue her own living and feeling as if her every financial decision was being weighed and judged, Olivia became frustrated and depressed. Warren didn't even know his behavior had affected her so much until coming home from a business trip to find both her and the baby gone.

For many couples, managing their finances becomes synonymous with managing their spouses. Although money can sometimes denote control, relationships should never be about one partner trying to dictate the other's behavior.

Points to Ponder

1. Does your spouse try to budget your spending and not his or her own? How does that make you feel? Are you likely to spend more as a result or, the opposite, worry about every expense?

   _____

2. Has your partner ever demanded an account of your expenditures even when there's no evidence of overspending? If yes, have you tried finding out what brought on this behavior?

   _____

3. Do you constantly agonize over purchases because you fear your partner's disapproval? If yes, how does this anxiety affect your everyday life?

   _____

Warning Sign #3: Frustration with Roles

One of the most common and easily remedied mistakes couples make before taking their vows is failing to outline the financial roles they will play in the marriage. We come into marriage with a unique set of expectations concerning our parts in the financial equation, expectations that can differ drastically from those of our spouses. For example, if you want to stay home and take care of the kids and your spouse expects you to go to work, you can begin discussing your financial roles early in the relationship to avoid confusion. Not only that, but you have to account for the fact that your role may change in a marriage and stay flexible in times of turmoil and role reversal.

A marriage is much like a business partnership. Both parties are held accountable for their actions, and are expected to contribute to the growth of the enterprise. In an ideal setting, business partners don't often get frustrated with each other's contributions. Each has skills and abilities that complement the other's, and they know it. For example, in many business situations, one partner brings in new clients, while the other handles marketing and financing. Each has a vital role to play in furthering the common cause. The most important thing to remember is that the partners have to be satisfied with their role and respect the other's contribution.

Andrea, a 28-year-old office manager, came to see me to file for a divorce from her husband of three years. They had one child, a little girl named Kelly, and I could tell that Andrea was very distressed about making the decision to get a divorce. Andrea married Michael after she discovered that she was pregnant with their daughter. At the time, she was working as a file clerk at a law firm. She and Michael had planned on getting married, and the baby served to catalyze their decision. The two were very much in love.

"After the wedding, I quit my job," Andrea began. "Michael was very supportive of me. He had talked about wanting to take care of me so I could raise a family and didn't seem to mind being the sole provider. I just assumed that he would want me to stay home with Kelly after she was born. But after a year, Michael became really frustrated. I don't know if it was his job or what. There was talk of layoffs.

"All I know is that he started complaining about finances, and would tell me how I should think about getting a job and contributing. As if I didn't do practically everything for him—wash his clothes, pick up his dry cleaning, get the car tuned up, you name it, not to mention everything I did for the baby. He just didn't have any respect for me or what I was doing. The complaints became more frequent as time went on. Michael treated me like I was lazy for staying at home, and I became more and more defensive about my role. That's when I decided to get a job. Even though I hated it, I accepted the offer just to spite him. And that's when the trouble really began."

Needless to say, Jane and Michael grew to resent each other until both had decided that they were tired of each other. But it wasn't until after Jane had filed for divorce that Michael became very apologetic, pleading for her to rethink her decision. After some serious and in-depth conversations, they were able to figure out that the relationship wasn't working for the simple reason that each had no idea about the pressures the other was facing. Once Michael explained to Andrea about his job stresses and financial worries, she became more understanding and supportive of his role. Michael, too, developed a newfound respect for Andrea's work around the house. After following her around for one afternoon from one chore to another, he quickly learned just how difficult household management could be. The couple eventually reached a compromise. Andrea would work part-time and Michael promised to help out around the house.

During the days of the single-income family, marriage partners had a better understanding of each other's roles. One would take care of the family and household, and the other would earn a living to support the family. Of course, that way of life had its limitations and created its own set of difficulties. But the simplicity of that arrangement is undeniable. Modern households are now forced to evaluate what roles each partner plays in a marriage. Because there is not one standard economic structure, each couple has to figure out what works for them. And although you may not believe that establishing individual responsibilities is important, couples, like business partners, need to have an intrinsic understanding, value, and respect for what each is bringing to the table in order for the marriage to be successful.

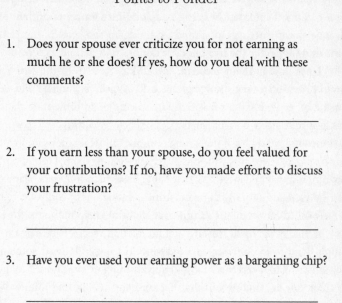

Points to Ponder

1. Does your spouse ever criticize you for not earning as much he or she does? If yes, how do you deal with these comments?

   _____

2. If you earn less than your spouse, do you feel valued for your contributions? If no, have you made efforts to discuss your frustration?

   _____

3. Have you ever used your earning power as a bargaining chip?

   _____

Money: Crimes and Misdemeanors

Crime and Misdemeanor #1:
Holding On to Your Holdings

When Angela, one of New York's famous socialites (the kind you hear about regularly in the gossip columns) came into my office, she was visibly angered. She was calling her husband, Rudolf, an accomplished photographer, every conceivable name. It was only when I calmed her down and asked her to tell me her story that I understood.

Rudolf was always flying off to one exotic location shoot after another. As the photographer of the moment for the leading fashion magazines, he was always in demand and was booked months, sometimes years, in advance. Angela admitted that although her marriage had its share of troubles, rumors of other women, and so on, Rudolf had always been extremely kind and attentive to her. She couldn't remember the last time they had fought. Angela also admitted to liking the lifestyle that being married to Rudolf afforded her. The couple resided in an important Park Avenue apartment, kept a famously extravagant residence in the Hamptons, and were often the most notable donors at local fund-raisers.

"I had just brought Stephan, my Yorkie, back from the hairstylist, when I received a very strange phone call," Angela recounted. "The voice on the other end had a thick German accent. He informed me that the bank would need a confirmation code before closing an account. I assumed they had gotten the wrong number, but when they said my husband's name, I became suspicious. After questioning them, I found out the account number and location of the bank. It was in the Cayman Islands. To calm myself and stop my thoughts from spiraling out of control, I immediately called Howard, our accountant. He would help me get to the bottom of this. When I told Howard that Rudolf had a secret bank account, he didn't deny it. He just kept stammering. He finally blurted something about having to take a meeting, and quickly hung up the phone."

For Angela, finding out that her husband was hiding money from her was extremely traumatic. It wasn't so much a matter of money, but of trust. She felt betrayed. What's more, uncovering that one secret made her wonder what else Rudolf had been hiding. According to reports that surfaced soon after she filed for divorce, Rudolf had over $10 million dollars stashed away in separate off-shore accounts. And although Rudolf tried to reconcile with her, explaining that the money had been relocated for tax purposes, Angela refused to get back together. She couldn't imagine living with someone as deceptive and calculating as her soon-to-be-ex-husband.

You don't have to be a millionaire to conceal money from your spouse. I have known many households, both wealthy and middle class, in which one spouse hides money from the other. And although a couple may be able to bounce back from this, concealing money from your spouse is one of the surest and fastest ways to end a marriage. Not only does it establish an irreparable divide between you and your spouse, but it destroys the trust that is crucial to establishing a partnership. Even if your spouse never needs for anything and you manage to provide for them to the best of your ability, concealing your net worth will introduce the kind of problems that few people are ever prepared to deal with. Most important, think about why it is you mistrust your spouse in the first place and make an effort to rebuild the trust before suspicions escalate on both sides.

Points to Ponder

1. Have you ever tried to conceal financial information from your spouse? Yes _____ No _____
   If yes, think about why you do this. Fear of criticism or distrust of your spouse?

   _____

2. Do you always keep your partner informed of investments and bank transactions?

   _____

3. Have you ever suspected your partner of hiding financial assets? Yes _____ No _____
   If the answer is yes, have you communicated your suspicions to your spouse?

   _____

Crime and Misdemeanor #2:
Spending Frivolously

In my opinion, frivolous spending is anything involving the purchase of luxury items without your spouse's consent. While you wouldn't want to go into all of the details concerning your day-to-day expenses (meals, cab rides, clothes), you should make a habit of consulting your partner before buying anything of significant value, like a car, real estate, expensive jewelry, or the like. Although this should go without saying, you'd be surprised at just how often people conveniently forget to consult their spouses. Besides causing financial strain, failing to inform your spouse of important financial decisions communicates that you have little respect for his or her opinion. In the end, your spouse won't resent the expense nearly as much as the fact that it was decided upon without his or her consent.

Trudy, a buyer for a large department store, was the kind of woman who would rather die than be caught wearing anything from a past season. She came to me after finding herself on the receiving end of her husband's wrath for repeatedly making large purchases without his consent. Although she was aware of having been at fault, she still adamantly defended her position.

"Asking Ben for anything was like pulling teeth. He would get a pained expression on his face, and look at me as if I had just grown a horn in the middle of my head. I tried to explain why I needed the new Fendi clutch and Gucci trench, but he just didn't understand. It was all for work. I can't very well be an accessories buyer for the most prestigious department store in the United States without conveying the right image. And it wasn't as if Ben couldn't afford it. I think he just didn't want me to be happy."

Although I understood the logic of Trudy's argument, I couldn't help but sympathize with her husband Ben, who worked as a strategic consultant to major corporations. During a deposition, he voiced his concerns about his wife's erratic spending habits. He even offered up their last credit card statement with a balance that exceeded the $30,000 mark as evidence. From the sad expression on his face, I gathered that Ben was still in love with his wife, but could simply not afford to keep the marriage going. Trudy, on the other hand, showed little emotion about the disruption of her marriage. In fact, soon after a settlement was reached, I spotted her shopping at Saks with another gentleman.

Although Trudy bounced back fairly quickly, most people would probably have a harder time recuperating from a divorce. I remember another less affluent client, Janet, who supported her husband, Bill, while he completed law school. Not only was she forced to work overtime as a nurse, she also had mounting debts from her husband's exorbitant spending habits.

"I loved Bill very much and would have done anything for him, except that he was the kind of person that the more you did for him, the more he came to expect. After school, he would often go out with friends, while I would be begging for extra late-night shifts at the hospital. I thought I was doing the right thing helping him get through law school, but soon I began receiving all these bills from the credit card companies. He would spend hundreds of dollars buying beers for his friends. I didn't know what had happened to our marriage, but I kept plodding along hoping Bill would see the error of his ways and straighten out. So when he came home to tell me that he was quitting school to find himself and would I please support him through this difficult time, I knew that I had supported him long enough and called it quits."

The couple divorced when Bill quit law school, without any intention of finding a job or helping his wife pay for his own debts.

You have to ask yourself what your marriage is worth to you. If it doesn't come close to the joy you feel when buying a new necklace or a new stereo system, then you may in fact be ready for a divorce. But if you feel that all the luxury items in the world couldn't replace your spouse, by all means curb the spending and work on creating a sound financial plan that both you and your spouse can stick to.

Points to Ponder

1. Do you often buy items on impulse?

   _____

2. Has your spouse ever complained about your overspending?

   _____

3. Do you feel that your partner is incapable of controlling his or her spending?

_____

Crime and Misdemeanor #3:
Folding Under Pressure

Why is it that even the most well-adjusted people can be a little weird when it comes to money? Whether you're a CEO of a company or a custodian, you probably have issues connected with money that go much deeper than your pockets, issues such as security, control, and self-worth. Although money is important to your family's well-being, it's just as important that you maintain perspective and never let money become the central issue. Once that happens, we tend to lose sight of what really makes our world go round.

June and Ronald had been married for over ten years when he lost his lucrative job as the head of investor relations at a large public company. Until that point, the couple had no financial problems to speak off. They dined at the finest restaurants in New York, lived in an ivy-coated brownstone on the Upper West Side, and sent their son to one of the best private schools in New York. While Ronald went off to work each day, June spent most of her time organizing charity events and setting up housing and educational programs for disadvantaged youth.

They were the very picture of domestic tranquility, except for one glaring fact: Besides their love of the good life, June and Ronald had very little in common. Due to separate vacations and sleeping quarters, the couple managed to see very little of each other despite having been married for ten years. Still, according to June, the strong feelings that brought them together in the first place were still there and allowed them to continue the marriage. "I sometimes thought no matter how much he worked or how many vacations he missed, we would always end up together," explained a distracted June, while looking out the window of my office. "We knew about the merger well in advance, but Ronald always talked about it as if it was a good thing. He even spoke of getting a promotion. Only a week after the merger was completed, Ronald was asked to hand in his resignation. Neither of us could believe it. He gave twenty years of his life to that company. At first, Ronald stayed calm. I think he thought that I was close to unraveling. He just assumed that I would be harder hit by the news, and never bothered to really think about the implications of his dismissal. He kept trying to convince me that we were okay . . . that I wouldn't have to worry about anything. More than anything, I think he was probably trying to convince himself.

"It couldn't have been more than a week since he'd lost his job that I came into the living room to find him weeping on the floor. I had never seen him so emotional before. When I reached out to him, asking him what was wrong, he went on a long tirade about how pressured he felt about supporting me and our son, how he was sure he would never get another job . . . he basically told me we were ruined. I have never seen anyone so panicked before."

June and Ronald's saga ended with June having to pack her belongings and move in with her mother. Ronald's inability to cope with the changes in his fortune left her no choice. He wouldn't look for another job, refused to seek mental health counseling, and was convinced that he was the biggest failure in the world. Panic had gotten the best of him, and instead of taking constructive steps to fix the problem, he became unmotivated, lethargic, and contentious with everyone he met.

Of course, leaving Ronald during this time was extremely difficult for June. She couldn't help but feel that she was abandoning her husband during his time of need. To her credit, however, she made every effort to get help for Ronald and even offered to go to work herself. Still, nothing panned out.

There will always be times of financial instability. One day you feel as if there will always be money to spare, and the next you begin to think that you will never have enough to get by. When people's main source of financial income is obstructed or threatened in some way, their first reaction is to panic. They begin to worry that they will become destitute and will never find another stream of income. But as most of us have learned, when you're down, you have nowhere to go but up, provided you stay calm and try to come up with new ways of supporting your family.

Points to Ponder

1. How well do you cope with financial setbacks? Are you most likely to formulate a plan or spend time worrying about the problem?

   _____

2. Have you ever acted irrationally when confronted with monetary pressures? Please explain.

   _____

3. Is your spouse able to maintain composure in the face of rising costs, mounting bills, and increased debts? If no, what kind of behavior have they exhibited during these times?

   _____

Money: Effecting a Reconciliation

Reconciliation #1: Get Informed

My first impression of Jannika, a onetime model, was that money was the least of her concerns. She walked into my office looking immaculate, like she'd just come from lunch at Daniel, a five-star restaurant in New York. I certainly wouldn't have pegged her problems as financial. Of course, that in itself was the problem.

"I always thought that our finances were very easy to manage," Jannika explained. "As a venture capitalist, Roger made more than enough money to support our lifestyle. We lived and vacationed in the most desirable locations, denied ourselves nothing, and never used public transportation. Then, about a year ago, Roger started acting a bit strange. He began talking about selling our home in Palm Beach, saying that we hardly ever use it. I love the area and our house there, so I flat-out refused. A few months later, I noticed that Roger got testy when he saw me wearing a new watch. A week ago, I answered the phone and took a message from a Florida realtor. Roger had sold our Palm Beach home without telling me.

"No wonder the sight of my watch upset him—it cost $25,000 if it cost a cent. What upset me, though, was Roger's secrecy. He should have just told me about our financial situation instead of allowing me to go around looking like a fool in front of all my friends. Clearly, everyone knew about our financial problems but me."

After hearing this story, I couldn't believe Jannika could have remained so blind to the reality of her financial situation. In retrospect, I think her appointment with me was a rash act, made hastily and in the face of great frustration. In fact, she told me that her husband was wonderful in every way and that were it not for this last act of betrayal, she'd never be contemplating divorce.

It was obvious that Jannika didn't need a lawyer so much as time to adjust her eyes to the light of truth. I told her that I'd be glad to represent her, but that I thought a divorce was premature in this case. Sensing that Jannika was nowhere near as angry with her husband as with herself, I suggested she try to take a more active role in financial planning and see what happened. When she left my office, she seemed genuinely excited about the prospect of getting involved and taking a more hands-on approach to her finances. The other night, I actually ran into Jannika at a benefit. She introduced me to Roger, her husband of eighteen years.

Although Jannika and Roger's was not a dual-income household, I have seen many dual income marriages suffer because one of the parties simply can't be bothered with the bills, stock portfolio, real estate investments, or bank accounts. This kind of laissez-faire attitude is all right when finances are in order; but should money problems ever arise, it almost always leads to resentment on the part of the spouse who is charged with the weighty task of handling all the fiscal duties; and to shock, anger, and feelings of disappointment on the part of the formerly "disinterested" spouse.

Before you end up blaming your partner for squandering all your hard-earned money, I suggest you take a long, hard look at your financial situation. Then and only then will you be able to act accordingly.

Exercise: How Well Do You Know Your Finances?

Finding out exactly how informed you are about your finances is not only important to your peace of mind, it will make you a better and more capable money manager. By letting your spouse make financial decisions for you, you are communicating that you cannot be bothered with the details of your marriage. And although money management may seem like a hassle at first, the rewards of keeping track of your holdings are immeasurable for you and your spouse.

1. Between you and your spouse, how much money do you have in the bank right now?

   _____

2. What kind of accounts are they (checking, savings, or both)?

   _____

3. If you have a stock portfolio, list some stocks you have recently bought and sold.

   _____

4. To the best of your ability, write down how much money you have in your checking account, savings account, and various investments.

   _____

5. What was the last bill you paid?

_____

6. How much debt do you have?

_____

7. If you own a home, what is the interest rate on your mortgage?

_____

Reconciliation #2: Learn to Budget

I always say that a trial separation is just practice for a real divorce. The fact is, you don't get back together by separating. The case of Cheryl and Sylvio, however, proved to be an exception. Today, the couple's marriage is stronger than ever, and it's my sincere belief that they have their financial acumen to thank for much of their current good fortune. To begin with, Cheryl, a landscape architect in her late forties, and Sylvio, a 50-something university professor, came to discuss getting a divorce together, as a team. They were having problems rekindling the spark in their marriage and had grown apart with the years. Neither had any worries about being "taken to the cleaners" by the other during the divorce proceedings. When I heard about the way they'd structured their finances during their marriage, I quickly understood why.

Despite their less than astronomical incomes, the couple had managed to amass substantial wealth. What was most unique, though, was that both Cheryl and Sylvio were in complete accord when it came to dividing their worldly possessions. "Cheryl's always been so good with money," Sylvio said. "She's the mastermind behind all of our good investments, as well as the budget that allowed us to save enough money to make these investments in the first place."

The trust and understanding between the couple was a natural response to having budgeted together throughout their many years as husband and wife. Because of the good fiscal planning that enabled them to save so much, they had always been aware of each other's financial needs and spending habits.

At the conclusion of our initial meeting, Cheryl and Sylvio opted to forgo an immediate divorce in favor of a trial separation. They even tried dating other people for a while. In the end, what stands out is what Sylvio said to me right before moving back in with Cheryl: "Bob," he said, "I've been meeting a lot of very nice women, but I'm not sure I could trust any of them the way I trust Cheryl."

Evidently, a sound budget is as crucial to a happy marriage as it is to a robust bottom line. Budgeting as a couple helps develop trust, admiration, and mutual respect within the relationship, not to mention the wonders it does for your children's college funds, your retirement fund, and your state of mind in times of financial uncertainty.

Of course, I have seen many couples ravaged by dwindling finances and incapable of planning, much less implementing, new budget-related initiatives. The problem is that most people see budgeting as a constraint on their individual freedom. They resent having to account for every dollar, and look enviously upon those people who can afford to spend lavishly without thinking twice. Some of my clients have complained about the rigidity and strictness of their budgets. Many more have even gone on to file for a divorce on the grounds that their spouse uses budgeting to control their spending, and, ultimately, their lives. Still, a sound budget can mean the difference between a comfortable and stable life and perpetual anxieties about the future.

The first key to successful budgeting is to prepare a financial plan that is mutually satisfying to both partners. In order to do that, you have to account for one another's spending habits. For instance, if your husband is a spender and you're the saver, make an effort to allot a little more each month for his expenses. Doing this will prevent your spouse from feeling cut off financially, and overspending as a form of rebellion. You can also work in an incentive plan that offers a bonus if your spouse sticks to the budget. By looking forward to more purchases later, your spouse may make an extra effort to curb his or her spending habits.

Reconciliation #3: Set Weekly Financial Meetings

While some couples have an easier time separating love and finances, others feel as if their marriage is all business. Catherine, a top Manhattan real estate broker, came to see me about a divorce. She was very concerned about her husband's attitude toward their joint assets, and was beginning to think that their marriage had become nothing more than a business arrangement. Kyle was the kind of man who was forever compensating for a disadvantaged childhood. As the head of his department at one of New York's best hospitals, he made a very good living, but was always squandering his income on status symbols, including multiple private club memberships, new cars (a BMW for himself and a Jaguar for his wife), custom-made suits, and the like. Despite having ample funds flowing in, the couple was incapable of holding on to their money and building up their savings.

"I don't know how people ever save any money," relayed a disgruntled Catherine. "No matter how much we make, there never seems to be enough. And yet everything we purchase is necessary to our way of life. There's the constant gift-giving for birthdays and weddings, the charity events, and a myriad of other expenses. We never really budgeted, but it got to the point that we began spending more than we were earning. That's when Kyle took matters into his own hands. He would constantly tell me about how much he was spending, investing, and depositing. I was required to do the same. It got to be so that we couldn't even have a dinner alone together without discussing what we needed and what we could do without. Every conversation had something to do with money. We went from one extreme to the other—from being completely oblivious to being painfully aware."

Although sticking to your budget and being aware of spending is crucial to successful money management, being too vigilant can make you feel as if your marriage is running on mutual monetary concerns rather than a mutual love for one another. The most effective way of keeping financial dealings and your love life separate is to schedule weekly thirty-minute meetings—a session in which both you and your spouse will be able to discuss anything from debt and bounced checks to overspending and new purchases. Once you've made this appointment, it will be very important to commit yourself to only discussing financial concerns during that time. There are millions of couples like Catherine and Kyle who, out of habit or anxiety, do nothing but argue or rehash their financial situation. But you will be surprised at just how much progress you can make during a weekly meeting, as well as the positive effects that isolating your financial talks will have on the quality of your marriage.

Exercise: Meeting Points

Setting a financial meeting agenda is critical to engaging in a productive exchange with your spouse. Make sure that both of you prepare a list of talking points or objectives that you would like to accomplish before you even sit down to discuss your finances. The following worksheet will help you organize your thoughts and address key financial issues.

1. How closely are you sticking to your budget?

   _____

2. Are you meeting your financial objectives?

   _____

3. Are there any large purchases that need to be discussed?

   _____

4. Have there been any financial setbacks in the past week?

   _____

5. Are you satisfied with the allocation of your funds?

   _____

6. Are there any financial investments you would like to make or change?

Reconciliation #4: Establish Mutual Financial Goals

Richard, a 36-year-old computer whiz, never seemed as though he knew where he was heading. Contrary to all appearances, however, he was in fact extremely driven and motivated to succeed. His wife, Mary, a petite woman with short brown hair, was exactly the same way. According to Richard, they had everything in common: their sense of humor and love of play and adventure, as well as the desire to start their own video game design company. Soon after graduating from college, Richard and Mary opened a small shop that eventually grew into a multimillion-dollar enterprise.

"For seven years Mary and I worked day and night to build the business. The company was successful early on, but we just couldn't assemble the right team. We were the only ones who knew what we wanted to achieve, and after going through many partners, it was decided that we would not let anyone else get involved in the business. Of course, the business didn't leave much time for anything else. We always talked about having a family, but only in the abstract. . . . Once we were more established.

"Generally, Mary and I were always on the same page. We understood one another like no one else. That's why I was so dismayed when our marriage began to fall apart. The trouble began right after we received a huge buyout offer from one of our main competitors. Mary became extremely elated, talking about how we could finally take a step back from the business and enjoy our lives. Personally, I thought we had been enjoying ourselves all along. It came down to Mary wanting to take the money and run, and me wanting to continue to grow and expand the company. I could see selling the company if I'd gotten into it just for the money. But it meant so much more to me than that. It was my whole life, and I thought Mary felt the same way."

As it turned out, Mary and Richard had very different financial goals. Although both had wanted to start a profitable business venture early in their marriage, Mary wanted to have a family even more. In her mind, the business was a way for her and Richard to make enough money so they could retire early and raise their children together. Unfortunately, in Richard's mind, the business *was* his baby. He derived a lot of satisfaction from running the company, and refused to let it go.

After a lot of arguing back and forth, the couple finally agreed to stay together. Through their numerous conversations, Mary and Richard came to see that a compromise might be better than a split. Because of their enduring love for each other and their willingness to reevaluate their financial and life goals, the couple decided to keep the business. Mary, however, would be free to stay at home and take care of the children that Richard agreed to have as soon as possible.

It's very easy to lose sight of the goals you and your partner share, and those you don't, especially when on the surface it seems as if you're in perpetual agreement. For instance, although both you and your spouse may be very responsible about saving money, you may have very different opinions on what you will do with your savings once the time comes to spend. While your spouse may want to save it to buy a new house, you may have considered using it to help your children later in life or for travel. So although you may be in agreement on the importance of saving, this is no guarantee that you'll always see eye to eye when it comes to money.

Talking about your financial goals and plans is one of the most important elements of successful money management. Assuming that you and your spouse are in agreement is just about the most dangerous thing you can do. The best way to maintain financial harmony is to spell out your objectives as clearly as possible. "Getting rich" or "saving money" just won't do. If you hope to continue living together in peace and harmony, you need to be as specific and as honest as possible with yourself and your partner.

Exercise: Personal Financial Goals

Since couples who share financial goals report less arguments regarding finances than those whose goals are at odds, it is important to establish a common ground early on in your marriage. The following exercise will help you determine the compatibility of your goals. If you find that you

don't have many financial goals in common, take time to analyze and outline the reasons behind your respective financial outlooks. Then you and
your spouse can sit down and reach a mutually agreeable compromise.

My Financial Goals

Goal 1: _____

Goal 2: _____

Goal 3: _____

Reason for goals 1, 2, and 3:

1. _____

2. _____

3. _____

Spouse's Financial Goals

Goal 1: _____

Goal 2: _____

Goal 3: _____

Reason for goals 1, 2, and 3:

1. _____

2. _____

3. _____

Common Financial Goals

Goal 1: _____

Goal 2: _____

Goal 3: _____

Money: Closing Argument

Signs that you're not coping with money to the best of your ability can arise at any time. It is critical to pay attention to cues that can alert you to bigger problems down the line. Money issues can creep up on the healthiest of marriages, but outlining your expectations and following a budget can significantly decrease your chances of divorcing over money.

When it comes to managing money, the most important thing to remember is that you are now part of a union, and every important decision needs to be reached unanimously. In my experience, most monetary dilemmas begin when people start making important financial decisions unilaterally, without first conferring with their spouse. Some of the most common money management mistakes made by couples include using money to control their partner's spending, not stopping to assess spending habits and money management styles early in the relationship, and disregarding conflicting financial goals.

One of the most important lessons you can take away from this chapter is that nothing about our attitudes toward money is normal. What works for your wife or husband will not necessarily work for you; what works for the couple next door will not make your finances run any smoother. You can, however, achieve financial harmony by customizing your budget and finances to fit both of your money management styles.

INFIDELITY

Infidelity can either destroy a relationship or be the first step toward mending one—that's up to the couple. Nevertheless, a significant portion of the divorce cases I've handled have resulted from a couple's inability to bounce back from infidelity.

Infidelity is kind of the universal whammy: It's so common that when a new client comes into my office and doesn't know why his or her spouse wants a divorce, I almost always make an inquiry to determine whether there is someone else.

Turn on the television, open a history book, read the newspaper, and you'll probably find some examples of infidelity. I'm sure you can think of at least five people you know who have had to cope with cheating partners at some point in their lives. As common a problem as infidelity may be, however, I must point out that by no means should it ever be viewed as "normal." Infidelity is the ultimate breach of trust between two people in a committed relationship. As such, it can wreak immeasurable damage and lead to tremendous, often insurmountable, familial discord.

Considering these disastrous repercussions, many of you are probably wondering why I decided to include infidelity in my list of seven *reconcilable* differences.

For a long time, I was convinced that if a spouse cheated, there was no going back. The breaking of trust, the lack of respect, the sheer dishonesty of the act—I wondered how any couple could ever hope to reconcile after such a serious infraction. How could anyone ever give a cheating spouse a second chance, much less learn to trust again? I found it hard to believe that any marriage, no matter how strong, could survive infidelity—until I met James.

A psychologist with his own private practice and a strong personality, James didn't strike me as someone who would put up with an adulterous wife. I thought then that the only people who stuck by a cheater were either desperate or in complete denial. James was neither. He walked into my office with an engaging smile and a firm handshake. After twenty years of marriage to his wife, Renée, a film producer, James was considering filing for a divorce.

"She's always been ambitious, argumentative, and strong-willed. I loved that about her. Most of all, I admired her opinionated nature. We challenged one another. Our passion came from always motivating one another to do better, to achieve more. Whenever one of us would lose that edge, that determination to be better, our relationship would suffer. I remember a time when one of my patients committed suicide. I couldn't sort it out, and started falling into a depression. Instead of babying me and tending to my every need, Renée demanded that I shape up. She knew that the moping would do me no good. She missed the old me, and, frankly, so did I.

"When it came out that she'd started having an affair, many of my friends rallied around me. 'How could she do that?' they protested. 'She doesn't deserve you.' I knew they were right, and decided to take steps to get out of the relationship. On the other hand, I couldn't help thinking about her and how much I still loved her."

By the time James had come in to see me, his friends and family had convinced him that he should sever the marriage, but listening to him tell it, I could see that he didn't really want to be anywhere near my office, let alone a courtroom.

"So how much of this decision is about what you want versus what everyone else thinks is right? What do you really want to do?" I asked James point-blank.

"I guess I need more time to figure it out," he sighed. And with that, he left my office, not to return for four months.

I had the pleasure of talking to James when he stopped by the office to say thanks and to wish me well. It was noon and we decided to grab something to eat. Over lunch, I carefully prodded him trying to figure out what had happened between him and Renée. Apparently, all was well.

"Despite what everyone told me about Renée—how selfish and uncaring she was—all I could think about was that I didn't deserve her. Instead of feeling like she let me down, I was convinced, and still am, that I had let her down by letting myself wallow in my misery. After thinking it over—and, believe me, I came close to calling it quits more times than you could imagine—I came to realize that the affair was a symptom of a bigger problem.

"It turns out that the man with whom she'd had the affair was very much like me before I became depressed. That's when I realized that she wasn't trying to leave me so much as to find the old me. And because I wasn't available, she sought out someone who would fill my shoes. In the end, it took the affair to jolt me out of my slump. I was determined to win her back. Having something else to worry about helped me forget about my own problems and resume my normal ways of life."

After weathering Renée's affair and James's depression, the marriage proceeded smoothly. It took an affair for James to realize that his wife's behavior was not about loving him less, but, in fact, about trying to get closer to him by being with someone who was more like James's original, more familiar personality.

Of course, not everyone whose spouse has an affair can be as pragmatic and reasonable as James. Rage, wounded pride, and jealousy keep most of us from ever facing up to the root causes of our partners' infidelity.

How well a couple bounces back from infidelity depends on a combination of factors, such as the couple's level of intimacy, commitment, communication, ego, and support. Although it may often seem that when infidelity is the problem, divorce is the only solution, the truth is hardly this cut and dried. From all that I've seen and heard, I know that there is hope for couples coping with infidelity, provided that the building blocks of a stable marriage are there. Of course the reasons may not always justify the behavior, but getting to the crux of the problem and finding a solution can help a couple survive the ordeal and build an even stronger relationship.

Infidelity Assessment

Assessing how you feel about infidelity, analyzing your issues with trust, and figuring out how you would cope with infidelity if it ever happened to you is critical to your marriage. Here are some questions to get you started:

1. Have you ever thought of cheating on your spouse? Have you ever acted on it? How do you think it would make your spouse feel to find out?

   _____

2. How would you feel if you found out that your spouse had feelings for someone else?

   _____

3. Do you think that your spouse is capable of having a one-night stand? What about a month-long affair?

   _____

4. Have you ever harbored suspicions that your spouse was having an affair? What did you do to find out?

   _____

5. Has your spouse ever been suspicious of you? How did he or she act on these suspicions?

   _____

6. Do you think you could ever forgive your spouse for having an affair? If yes, what conditions would you set?

   _____

7. Do you think your spouse would forgive you if you cheated?

_____

8. If you've ever cheated on your spouse, did you consider leaving your spouse for the other person? Yes _____ No _____
If yes, what qualities drew you to the other person? If no, what made you stay together?

_____

Infidelity: Warning Signs

Warning Sign #1: A Sudden Change in Daily Routine

A few years ago, Veronique, a model scout for one of the most prestigious agencies in New York, came into my office to begin divorce proceedings. A tall, slender woman with well-defined cheekbones and a stunning sense of style, Veronique was an ex-model who couldn't bear to part with the glamorous lifestyle she had become accustomed to as a young girl. Her husband, Kenneth, was a well-known architect in a large New York firm. They had been married for four years when Veronique became aware of a sudden change in his daily routine.

"Every day for about two and a half years, Ken would leave the house at about 8:00 A.M., grab some coffee from a street vendor, and find a cab that would take him to work. He would call me once before lunch, and then right before he was getting ready to go home. At night, we would arrive home at about the same time, and if I didn't have an event to go to, we would stay home and make sushi. Our lives pretty much ran like clockwork.

"About three months ago, I noticed that Kenneth was beginning to work longer hours. His phone calls also became less regular. Some days he would call twice, other days once, and, on a number of occasions, not at all. When he would come home late, he always had the same excuse: The company had downsized and he had to take on a lot more work. For a time, I believed him. But gradually I became more and more suspicious. One time, at one of Kenneth's corporate functions, I asked the company president to explain why they'd had to cut so much staff. And he just looked at me with this blank expression on his face, like he had no idea what I was talking about.

"That's when I panicked and hired a private investigator. He suggested that we trace all of my husband's local phone calls. I never knew that this was even an option, and quickly agreed to it. I didn't even think about what I could find. The idea that Kenneth may have been cheating on me never even occurred to me. When the investigator conducted the trace, he found that Kenneth had made over a hundred calls in one month to the same number. Through a reverse directory, he found the address, and waited for Kenneth to show up at the door. That's when he took pictures of Kenneth and another woman walking arm in arm toward her house. It was obvious what was going on."

Soon after, Veronique became obsessed with her husband's affair. Instead of confronting Kenneth, she became so paranoid that she would actually follow him around wearing a wig and big glasses. She also admitted to checking his bills and phone records daily. It dawned on me that she had stopped trying to prove that her husband *was* having an affair and had begun trying to prove that he *wasn't*. There was something very touching about her story. It was obvious that she was still very much in love with him. In truth, the more she chased him around town, the more she loved him.

When I asked her to think about what was at the root of her behavior, she was a little taken aback by my insinuation that she still had strong feelings for Ken. But slowly, during our conversation, she became more comfortable and admitted to wanting to make the relationship work, provided, of course, that Ken sever his extramarital relationship immediately.

Fortunately, Ken was just as adamant about putting the infidelity behind them. He had been begging Veronique for a second chance all along. The couple had a lot of issues to work out and were in counseling for months. When I ran into Veronique at a restaurant opening and heard about how well she and Ken were progressing, it was obvious the effort had not been a waste of time.

In the end, it was Veronique's vigilance that brought the infidelity to the forefront. Only then was the couple able to tackle their problems head-on and forge a stronger union. The lesson here is that no matter how seamless your partner's excuses, a change in routine should always send up a red flag in your mind. Even if the excuse is valid, like a change of job or a relocation, a little paranoia can be a good thing if it makes you aware of your partner's day-to-day activities.

What's most important is that you don't become so preoccupied with your spouse's comings and goings that you become overly guarded, anxious, and suspicious. Striking the right balance between healthy concern and extreme paranoia isn't difficult, provided you keep your suspicions reigned in until you find that you actually do have something to worry about.

Points to Ponder

1. Does your spouse adhere to a regular daily routine?

   _____

2. Have you noticed any sudden changes in your partner's routine?

   _____

3. Has this change made you suspicious?

   _____

4. Could factors (promotion, relocation, etc.) other than infidelity account for this change?

   _____

Warning Sign #2: Acting Defensive

Anthony, a middle-aged lawyer, had been having an affair with his legal assistant, Jessica, for over two years. His wife, Melinda, had never realized that he was involved in anything extramarital until she showed up at his office late one night to surprise him when he was working late. Upon walking into his office, she was shocked to find him having sex with the assistant. When she questioned her husband and found out the duration of their relationship, she immediately demanded a divorce.

"The affair started almost immediately," Anthony explained. "I thought we would have some fun, and that would be the end of that. I never expected the relationship to last. When I tried to break it off with my girlfriend, Jessica, I realized that I couldn't live without her. I was too much in love. I think Jessica knew what I was going through, and decided to use my feelings to her advantage. She would constantly ask me when I was planning to leave my wife, and would get mad when I stalled her. The truth was that no matter how much I loved Jessica, I was too dependent on Melinda. We had built a life together, and my kids would never have forgiven me.

"Anyway, I continued the affair for two years because I simply couldn't bring myself to end it. I couldn't say no to Jessica, and I couldn't leave my wife. I was stuck. About three months into the whole thing, I began feeling very guilty and angry for getting myself into such a mess. But instead of doing something about it, I became very difficult to be around. I was angry, restless, and defensive. I was always worried that my wife would find me out. Melinda and I couldn't have a conversation without me acting out in some way. I almost hoped she would catch on to my strange behavior. I wanted to get caught so I could find a way out of the situation I was in. All the signs were there, but Melinda never picked up on any of them."

Ever notice how defensive people become when they are caught telling a lie or when they feel that someone is trespassing on their territory? That defensiveness is what cheaters have to live with on a daily basis. Their lives consist of one cover-up after another, feelings of guilt, and the fear that they will someday be discovered. All of this can add up to a lot of nervousness and anxiety, which will in turn cause the cheater to become defensive and agitated at the slightest provocation. Of course, not all defensive people can be automatically relegated into a cheaters category. You have to use your common sense. However, if questions like, "Where have you been?" and "Where are you going?" elicit a strong reaction from your spouse, it's likely that they are indeed keeping something from you.

It's also interesting to note the role that denial played in the relationship. Melinda must have been aware of her husband's irritability and late nights at the office, but chose not to probe or ask questions. It was as if she was scared to face the truth. Had she simply asked some questions or tried to get to the root of her husband's erratic moods, Anthony might have admitted to having the affair sooner rather than later. Because the infidelity was allowed to continue unchecked for as long as it did, Melinda was even more upset when the facts were revealed. Had Melinda discovered the affair earlier, she and Anthony might have stood a better chance of bouncing back and becoming a stronger couple.

Ask and You Shall Learn

Getting the truth out of your partner can be as easy as posing a few relatively unassuming questions and carefully gauging your partner's response. Just remember: What your partner says is not nearly as important as what he or she does. Pay close attention to his or her feelings and emotions, and be extra vigilant if your partner:

- cannot look you straight in the eye

- immediately gets defensive

- fidgets and cannot stand still

- tries to change the subject

- does not answer your questions

- takes times to think about a response

- responds in a way that seems overrehearsed

- provides too much detail

Warning Sign #3: Providing Too Much Information

Glenn, a business consultant and popular keynote speaker, was a distinguished-looking man who felt that his success depended upon his professional image. Sheryl, his wife of six years, was a dermatologist who wound up getting involved in an ongoing relationship with one of her patients.

"Sheryl was always a little high-strung after work. I would ask her where she'd been and what she'd done, and she would provide me with the most detailed and long-winded explanations of her adventures. Everything from who she saw, to what they were wearing, to the drinks and food she consumed was described in the most elaborate detail. Normally, I would simply sit back and listen attentively to her explanations. I thought that taking so much time to recount her whereabouts was a sign that my wife loved me, and wanted me to be a part of her life.

"The stories became a vital part of my life. I never thought to question why Sheryl told me so much about her life when a simple explanation would have sufficed. Apparently, the fear of getting caught made Sheryl a little too good of a storyteller. Her tales had become so elaborate that even she had a hard time keeping all her facts straight. There were a few times when I would ask her to repeat what she had told me the night before, and she would either forget or change the subject.

"I guess it was getting difficult for Sheryl to keep coming up with new scenarios because she finally told me about the affair. The funny thing was, when Sheryl opened up about her relationship, I wasn't a bit surprised. It was as if I knew all along but just refused to pay attention to what was going on."

When Glenn approached me about filing for divorce, we discussed his situation in detail. Every time I asked him about his past, what he wanted to get out of the divorce, he would wince visibly, as if he was still not reconciled to the idea of divorce. The word alone made him uncomfortable. When I asked about Sheryl's affair and if it was still going on, Glenn waited a few minutes and told me that she had ended the relationship and was calling him every day trying to patch things up.

I suggested that he take some time to think about what he was getting into. I also suggested that he talk to his wife and come to terms with the emotional impact that the affair had had on him. And if he still wanted to get a divorce after doing all that, I told him to come and see me. Last I heard, Glenn and Sheryl had put the past behind them, and had relocated to Los Angeles.

There are those people who say very little for fear of getting caught, and others who say way too much, hoping that their detailed accounts will create a diversion. If your spouse has a tendency to exaggerate or provide answers to questions you never posed, you may want to pay special attention to what is going on in their lives. Once again, providing detailed, in-depth accounts of their daily lives doesn't mean your partner is cheating on you. There are some people who like to tell stories, and are very forthcoming about the events in their lives. Still, if your strong, silent spouse suddenly turns into a chatty overcommunicator, you may want to think about the factors contributing to this change.

Never be afraid to uncover something potentially painful. It is important to gently probe your spouse if you suspect they are being unfaithful. The more time you allow the affair to go on, the worse the aftermath is likely to be. Even if your spouse is conducting an affair, there are many ways for a marriage to bounce back from infidelity if that is what both partners want. Crazy as it sounds, an affair does not have to signal an end.

Points to Ponder

1. Does your spouse normally tell you about his or her day in great detail? Yes _____ No _____

   _____

2. Does your partner introduce new people into his or her anecdotes without providing the necessary background information? Yes _____ No _____

   _____

3. Does you spouse become anxious when you ask him or her to repeat themselves? Yes _____ No _____

Warning Sign #4: Inability to Trust

For many couples dealing with infidelity in their lives, the question is not about how to prevent infidelity but how to cope with its inevitable fallout. How do I forgive my spouse? Is it possible to renew our commitment to the marriage? How can I ever trust again? These are the questions that haunt most of the people who've been hurt by infidelity.

Making the decision to stay together or divorce after an extramarital affair is only the first step to recovery. One indication that you may need more help coping with infidelity is a complete inability to trust your partner. Trudy, a 44-year-old art appraiser for a major auction house in New York, came into my office to talk about the details of her second marriage to Gary, a Broadway producer. She had been married before, but divorced when she discovered her husband had cheated on her. Apparently, in failing to resolve the issues that had arisen within her first marriage, she had unwittingly carried them into her second with Gary.

"I knew I was right not to trust him. I was sure something was wrong almost immediately, especially when he started working out. Whenever I tried to mention exercise to him before, he would scoff and make some flippant comment about what nonsense it all was.

"A couple of months ago, I began noticing changes. It started with him sleeping more each day. He would then get up in the morning and spend at least five minutes in the bathroom. When I walked past him one time, I noticed him staring in the mirror and trying to comb his hair. My first reaction was to laugh. I had never seen him take such pains with his looks. But I soon found out that this was no laughing matter.

"After three months of careful observation, I became convinced that he was having an affair. He had hired a private trainer to work with him at the theater and had instructed his assistant to only serve him fat-free, low-calorie lunches. I know because she joked about it with me one day over the phone.

"That's when I was sure he was having an affair. Not wanting to waste time, I decided to confront him immediately. I stormed into the theater and pulled him aside. 'I know everything,' I said. And then I asked him point-blank, 'Are you having an affair?' When he had the audacity to look me straight in the eye and say 'No,' I understood that I would have to be even smarter if I wanted to confirm the truth."

Trudy proceeded to recount some of the measures she took to catch Gary in the act, including snooping and making scenes wherever they went. She also explained that she and Gary began fighting more often. The more she pried into his personal life, the angrier he would become. Every time she would ask him if he was cheating on her, Gary would storm out of the room in a rage. After a while, he became so tired of the accusations that he started spending more time with friends than with her. It was then that he actually developed a brief relationship with another woman from one of his productions.

"I couldn't believe it when he told me. I thought he had been cheating on me all along, but now I feel like I drove him to it," she explained.

Like most couples, Trudy and Gary had a lot of baggage to sort through. There was a lot of anger, resentment, and guilt in their relationship, but there was even more love and attachment. Trudy was not ready to let go of their marriage, and Gary was equally lost without her.

It wasn't long before Trudy realized that she needed help getting past her fear of infidelity. She had been so hurt by her former husband's affair that she completely blocked out that part of her life until it crept back in without her knowledge. Once she came to grips with her role in Gary's affair, she understood that what she and Gary needed was a separation, not a divorce. During that time, Trudy worked hard to resolve her infidelity-related intimacy issues and the couple was able to resume their relationship with a better understanding of one another.

There are times when we think our old wounds have healed only to realize that they can reopen at the slightest provocation. The damage caused by infidelity cannot be undone with what I call a "Band-Aid" reaction. Making a firm decision to stay together or to separate is a good first step, but by no means does it indicate that a couple is finished working through the issues related to cheating.

Accusing your spouse of infidelity without any corroborating evidence is not only a sure way to destroy the trust in your marriage, but it can actually drive your spouse to cheat on you. Many people with whom I have spoken reported having an affair only after realizing that their spouse didn't trust them, the rationale being, "If my spouse is already convinced I'm having an affair, what difference does it make if I actually have one?" And although that line of reasoning is obviously flawed and dangerous, it illuminates the importance of one simple fact: Your spouse is innocent until proven otherwise.

Whether you've decided to work through your trust issues alone or with your partner, you have to be prepared for setbacks and misunderstandings along the way. If you're having trouble putting an affair behind you, you must take action. Avoid the passive-aggressive route and talk about your feelings with your spouse. Remember, the best way to counter a fear of betrayal is admitting it to yourself and to your spouse. Then and only then can you work together to build a foundation of trust and start anew.

Points to Ponder

1. Have you ever rifled through your spouse's personal possessions to find evidence of infidelity? What circumstances led up to this event?

   _____

2. Do you trust your spouse not to cheat on you? Why or why not?

   _____

3. Have you ever accused your spouse of cheating on you?
    What led up to this event?

    _____

Warning Sign #5: Unexpected Acts of Generosity

Glenda came to me a couple of weeks after discovering that her husband Jacques, the owner of a hair salon in the city, had been carrying on a two-year affair. This was one of my toughest cases yet. I had seen plenty of people crushed by infidelity, but Glenda surpassed all of them in her extreme pain and suffering. A successful real estate broker, Glenda was so distraught about the affair that she was unable to work and needed to see a mental health professional every single day. She had a hard time getting out of bed in the morning, and contemplated suicide on a weekly basis. On top of all that, her financial situation was precarious, and she needed to get a good settlement in order to maintain her old lifestyle.

"I never thought he was capable of such betrayal," she said. "We managed to raise two kids together, and just as I was getting ready to settle into a comfortable and quiet coexistence, I found out that he had been sneaking around behind my back. I can't explain the shock, especially because he had only recently become so attentive to me. I thought it was maybe because the kids had finally gone off to school. I was so pleased with his behavior toward me. A year ago, he began bringing me all of these gifts. One day he came home with an opal pendant that was just so beautiful. I asked him what was the special occasion, and he would tell me that it was just because he loved me. When he got me a new Louis Vuitton overnight bag, he told me it was because the business was doing well. Of course, I believed him. Why would any wife question her husband's love for her? He was constantly showing me how much I meant to him. It's ironic, but I was the happiest I had ever been during that time.

"What finally alerted me to his infidelity was a receipt I found hidden in his underwear drawer. It was for a new bracelet he had just bought me.

The price read $600. But right below it was another charge for that same exact amount. I knew it was the same item charged twice because the product code was identical. My first thought was that Jacques had been overcharged by mistake. I decided to settle the matter quickly and stopped by the jewelry store that very day. When I showed the salesperson the bracelet and told him about the double charge, he informed me that the buyer had indeed purchased two identical bracelets. That's when I lost it completely. I knew right away that the store clerk was telling the truth. But still I couldn't admit what had happened to me.

"The next day, I hired a private investigator. He told me to make a list of all of the gifts I had received. He tracked the purchases, and almost all of them had a double. He had bought me and his mistress the same gifts. I couldn't tell you how hurt I was. I collected all of the items, and burned what I could in the fireplace. By the time he got home that day, I was screaming. I was literally going crazy. I was so hurt, so embarrassed, so disappointed. He left me that same day. I think I must have cried for a whole week straight."

Guilt can make a cheating heart do funny things. It can make your spouse turn away from you or try to alleviate their guilt by heaping presents and attention on you. The important thing is to watch for behavioral swings. If your spouse has always had a habit of surprising you with expensive gifts, then consider yourself lucky. But if your spouse never gave you anything except on special gift-giving occasions like birthdays and anniversaries, and then suddenly presents you with an expensive token just to say "I love you," you should temper your initial glee by considering the circumstances behind their sudden generosity.

Points to Ponder

1. Does your spouse surprise you with gifts on a regular basis?
   Yes _____ No _____

2. Has your spouse been unusually affectionate? Describe his or her behavior?

_____

3. Does your spouse have mood swings that veer from extreme generosity to total self-absorption?
   Yes _____ No _____

_____

4. What factors could be contributing to this strange behavior?

_____

Infidelity: Crimes and Misdemeanors

Crime and Misdemeanor #1:
Withholding Sex from Spouse

When Gerald, a 35-year-old restaurateur, came into my office, he told me an interesting story about his wife, Linda, and the affair she had been carrying on with her boss. The couple had been married for a little over six years and had one child. Gerald had a stylish and polished look to him. He was the kind of guy who made it a point to know everyone, and to inform every patron that there was a three-week wait list even during slow periods. Linda, a public relations associate at a major fashion house, was a very attractive woman who, if she was three inches taller, could have been a supermodel.

"Men were always hitting on Linda. I knew that when I met her. I was never jealous or suspicious of her, even though I knew she could have had any guy she wanted. When Linda and I got married, it was because she was pregnant. It's not that I didn't love her, it was just that I was never ready for marriage before and the prospect of having a baby put everything in perspective. As soon as I became a father, I stopped staying out late, and hired a few promoters to keep the restaurants in the public eye.

"Meanwhile, Linda began working late at the office. She had always been very ambitious. We had a lot in common in that respect, but now that she was coming home late, she would refuse to have sex with me. As you can imagine, this threw me for quite a loop. There had never been a time when she didn't want to have sex. Even when she was pregnant, we were always sexually active. Linda was just that way. She always wanted to have sex, sometimes even more than me.

"So when she would come home from work, I would be right there making all the moves. I would get us dinner, get our daughter Amy ready for bed, put some nice music on, just to set the mood. But after we had the dinner and went through all the pleasantries, she was still not interested. Finally, I had had enough and asked her what was wrong. I guess I became a little angry because she started yelling right back at me, getting really argumentative, like she was trying to pick a fight with me. That's when it slipped out. She had the nerve to tell me that she had been sleeping with someone and didn't want to cheat on him—her boyfriend. She didn't want to cheat on her boyfriend with me—her husband. I couldn't believe it. To this day, I'm still having a hard time grasping the idea. In the end, it was her way of telling me that she had fallen out of love with me, and didn't want to keep up the ruse by sleeping with me."

The idea of cheating on one's lover with one's husband or wife may seem the height of insanity to anyone who has never been unfaithful. But if an extramarital relationship continues for a long period of time, some people may stop having sex with their spouse because they are more interested in making love with their new partner who, in fact, they feel a greater loyalty to. In such cases, reconciliation becomes nearly impossible because both partners must want to mend their relationship for the marriage to rebound.

Points to Ponder

1. Have you ever cheated on your spouse only to find out that sex with someone new was more satisfying?
Yes _____ No _____

_____

2. How did that realization affect your sex life with your spouse?

_____

3. Have you ever tried to avoid sex with your spouse because of an extramarital affair? Yes _____ No _____

_____

Crime and Misdemeanor #2:
Picking On Your Spouse

Donald, a forensic psychologist, had been married to Jennifer for three years. He was very well read and extremely intelligent, the kind of guy who could talk expertly on almost any subject. The problem, as he described it, was that he preferred quiet evenings to social outings. The couple resided in Brooklyn Heights, away from the hustle and bustle of Manhattan, in an old, Gothic church that had been converted into a condo. The marriage was the first for both. Despite all of his advantages, Donald never had much luck with women. He would become tongue-tied and embarrassed around them. But when he met Jennifer, he was extremely comfortable with her. She was very social and outgoing, and

Donald admired her for that. She, in turn, liked his quiet and pensive nature, and was in awe of his piercing intellect.

"We always managed to work things out. Jennifer understood my problem with crowds, and was very happy to stay at home listening to music and renting old classic films. She never minded staying in, or so I thought. About a year and a half into the marriage, Jennifer became restless. She started scouring the magazines, looking for cool bars and clubs to go to. She kept asking me to come, but when I told her that I wasn't interested, she would get mad at me and tell me that I was boring and predictable. I thought she was just going through a phase, but her desire to go out only increased. She began frequenting night spots without me, opting to go out with some friends from work instead. At night, she would come home and start yelling at me for being lazy and what she termed antisocial. I couldn't believe how different she had become. She had never minded my habits before."

After having to deal with Jennifer's strange behavior, which included staying out late and finding fault with everything he did, Donald grew suspicious. When his inquiries to mutual friends yielded no conclusive results, he decided to hire a private investigator to keep track of his wife's whereabouts. Sure enough, he soon received word of his wife's affair.

Jennifer had been gallivanting about with a young man who liked to have his fill of the good life. In order to maintain his VIP lifestyle, the young man spent his money freely and cavorted well into the morning hours. It turned out that the detective not only uncovered Jennifer's affair, but he also found out that her lover was cheating on her with three other women. When Donald found out that his wife was deceiving him, his anger was magnified by such an inappropriate choice. He now understood that his wife's constant complaints and appeals were an attempt to convert him into the man with whom she had been having an affair.

When a person decides to have an affair, he or she is usually in the throes of infatuation, feeling heady and excited. The idea of spending time with a new lover is so appealing that the cheating spouse often develops a hostility toward anyone who gets in the way of their time together—and that includes the noncheating spouse. Although some people feel guilty having to lie and sneak behind a partner's back, others may resent having to bend over backward to hide affairs. They may even begin to criticize their spouses for things that never bothered them before, leaving the mate confused, bewildered, and certainly in no mood to work things out once the infidelity is discovered.

If you find that your feelings for your lover have progressed past the purely physical, it's time to figure out what it is you want out of the relationship. Whereas people sometimes resort to infidelity as an indirect attempt to improve the state of their marriage, cheating is often also a means of escaping a loveless relationship. If you find that you feel closer to your lover than to your spouse, or experience an intense infatuation that lasts more than one month, you may be trying to tell yourself that your marriage is over.

Points to Ponder

1. Do you ever find yourself comparing your spouse to your lover? If yes, does the comparison put your spouse in a more negative or positive light?

   _____

2. Even if you're not having a sexual relationship outside the marriage, do you ever wish your spouse could be more like other people you're attracted to? What are some of the qualities you wish he or she had?

   _____

3. Does your spouse complain about your negative comments?

   _____

Crime and Misdemeanor #3:
Dredging Up the Past

I have seen many cases of couples stuck in the past. Incapable of letting go of some past wrong that was destructive to the marriage, they use their partner's past mistakes as weapons in times of marital conflict. When Greg, an advertising representative, came into my office to seek a divorce from Lisa, his wife of seven years, it was clear that the two of them had been through a tough ordeal that they were in the process of dragging out.

"Lisa found out that I was having an affair with a coworker almost three years ago. It was extremely painful. She hated me, and even walked out on me for a month. I called her every day until she finally decided to give me another chance. I swore that I would never cheat on her again, and she accepted my apology.

"The first few months were pretty tough. But we managed to get through it. An old family friend was really great about getting us to talk about our feelings and we really benefited from the long discussions about marriage, faith, and fidelity.

"Initially, we were really sensitive to one another's needs, and I made sure I gave Lisa enough space so she could forgive me slowly without feeling pressured. Eventually, Lisa's attempts to keep a level head and put the past behind us began to wane. I noticed a very gradual change. At first, she started asking me about my day at work. But it wasn't the questions; it was how and when she asked me. It was usually right after I did something like forgetting to pick up dinner or not calling when I'd said I would.

"Eventually, her behavior escalated to the point where we'd be arguing and she would bring up my past affair to throw it in my face. I understood that she was upset about what had happened and that I had been wrong, but I felt that she was trying to use the past against me.

"Instead of feeling guilty about the affair, I became self-righteous, thinking that Lisa was now just as out of line as I'd been. Not only that, but by constantly bringing up what had happened, she provided a constant reminder of a time when both of us were extremely unhappy and uncommunicative. Pretty soon, I shut down completely. I was too scared to do anything that would cause a fight for fear of what would happen."

From where I sat, it was obvious that Lisa had some issues to work through. I even ventured to add that I wished they had both given each other enough time to deal with the infidelity without hastily jumping back into the relationship. Something was obviously not working for the couple, but I could sense that they had painted themselves into a corner. Lisa would need more time to come to grips with the infidelity, and to decide if she wanted to move toward a better future or wallow in the bitter past. Ultimately, Greg would have to leave it up to her.

When I expressed some of my thoughts to Greg, he was very open to the suggestion. He and Lisa were still in turmoil over what had happened, and were as anxious as anyone to find a resolution. After six months of separation, Lisa decided to give the marriage another shot. And from what Greg has told me since, she has made peace with the past.

Points to Ponder

1. Has your spouse ever tried to shame you into doing something by bringing up a past infidelity? If yes, did his or her behavior spark an argument?

   _____

2. Do you feel you are judged unfairly based on a past infidelity? Yes _____ No _____
   Please explain how this makes you feel.

   _____

3. Have you ever tried to use a spouse's affair against him or her? Yes _____ No _____
   If yes, do you feel that this behavior is productive in the long run? Please explain.

   _____

Crime and Misdemeanor #4:
Engaging in Unprotected Sex

It seemed as though I had been reading about Jerry and Karen in the *Wall Street Journal* for years. They were two of the hottest Wall Street executives in the industry. Karen was an attractive blonde who had made a name for herself in the industry, and Jerry was born and raised in New York, which is why the couple ultimately chose to buy a second home on the East Coast.

It seemed like Jerry and Karen had it all. So when Jerry's business lawyer called my office to arrange a meeting I was both flattered and dismayed. On the one hand, I was pleased by the prospect of handling such a high-profile case and meeting him and his wife in person. Then again, I was disappointed that what I thought was a picture of marital bliss was a forgery.

It wasn't 10 minutes after coming into my office that Jerry began opening up to me. And I will never forget what he told me:

"Marriage was never something I was interested in. My parents went through a messy divorce. The last thing I wanted was to end up miserable like them. I had heard about Karen through work and thought that she was amazingly beautiful, but it wasn't until I ran into her at a function that I really got to know her as a person. For a while, I thought that our meeting was fated, that we were somehow meant to meet and help each other get to the top. From our first few dates, I was convinced that I had found my soulmate. We did crazy things, like flying off to Rio on a whim. A month later, we eloped and bought a place together in Malibu and another one in Greenwich Village.

"What I soon discovered was that Karen was much more ambitious than I was. Actually, I didn't know her at all. I often wondered if she was even the same person I married. Her big goal became launching a career as a financial reporter. But when a big deal fell through, she became difficult and overbearing. She was never happy.

"It got to the point where I didn't want to be with her at all. I still loved her for the person I thought she was when we first met, but she had changed too drastically. I felt alone, desperate, and in need of someone to reach out to. Still, I never expected to hurt her like I did."

Jerry engaged in a few short trysts. As he saw it, women were always throwing themselves at him, and he was only human after all. He'd never given his exploits much thought until one of the women called to tell him that she had contracted herpes. Jerry was understandably worried, and immediately went in for a medical checkup only to find out that he, too, had contracted the virus. Now Jerry had no choice but to tell Karen about what had happened. Worse yet, he had to tell her about the risk to which he'd exposed her. Suffice it to say that Karen did not take the news with anything akin to composure. She was extremely angry and threatened to take him for all he was worth. But after much persuasion, she agreed to a quiet and speedy divorce.

Cheating on your spouse is inexcusable. But what is even more appalling is when a partner exposes their spouse to sexually transmitted diseases by failing to practice safe sex. I cannot stress enough the complete and total devastation that can occur when a person finds out that their spouse not only doesn't care enough to be honest with them, but that they do not even care enough to protect their lives. The message that I am trying to relay is that if, despite your better judgment, you decide to have an affair, the least you can do is protect your spouse by protecting yourself.

Infidelity: Effecting a Reconciliation

Reconciliation #1: Talk It Through

As a society, we often blame the cheater. And rightly so. It's one thing to have marital problems, but an entirely different matter to act on those feelings by cheating on your spouse. Still, in my experience, I've found that cheating happens when one person is not getting what they need out of a relationship. That's why it's so important to keep a level head and really listen to your partner's reasons for committing infidelity. Of course, there are times when your partner will try to avoid accountability by blaming you for their affair. I suggest you keep that in mind as you listen to what your partner is really trying to say. Even if you can place 100 percent of the blame on your spouse, you will probably end up learning something about yourself in the process.

Ginny, a 30-something PR wizard, found out about her husband's affair through the grapevine. Ginny is one of the best connected young women in Manhattan. Her clients range from celebrities to restaurant owners to top national magazines. If there was a star-studded event in town, you could bet that Ginny was somehow involved. Getting access to the juiciest bits of gossip was her livelihood, but she never expected that one day the tables would turn.

Her husband, Remmi, the son of a famous designer, had met her at one of her events. He was drawn to her vivacious personality and business savvy, and she couldn't resist the power that his name and status wielded.

"A few years into the marriage, Remmi became very involved in his father's business," she said. "He was always being sent away to Italy, Morocco, and France for business trips. At first I went with him, but gradually the demands of my business prevented me from accompanying him. When one of my employees came to me with news of Remmi being spotted all over town with some 19-year-old model, I became enraged. There were even rumors that he had bought an apartment in her name, and was planning to leave me. My pride was really hurt. I felt that my career, my reputation, everything was on the line. I couldn't believe he had the audacity to embarrass me like that. It was really mortifying.

"When he returned from his month-long trip, I confronted him openly, screaming and yelling until my vocal chords nearly gave out. I accused him of trying to discredit me and make a fool of me. And that's when he turned the tables. He told me it was exactly because I was so selfish, ambitious, and materialistic that he had cheated on me. He told me that I never cared about him, and was only interested in what other people thought and what he could do for my career.

"My first impulse was to object, but after a moment of reflection, I realized that he was right. I was more concerned with my image than how his affair would affect our marriage. It actually made me think a lot about my feelings for him. I had always thought that I didn't care about him at all, but now I realized that there was more to our marriage than just convenience."

As it turned out, Ginny never wanted to get a divorce, but was simply going along with the idea to save her reputation. She had actually thought about contesting the divorce, but was scared to talk to Remmi about their chances of getting back together. After a few months, she was able to see her role in her husband's affair and realized that she would have to make some changes if she wanted to make the marriage work. It was then that she approached Remmi about a reconciliation. As it turns out, both of them were ready to start a life together and became more committed then ever to making their marriage work.

Most people who catch their spouse cheating are tempted to have their say. After all, aren't they entitled to vent their frustrations? Weren't they the injured party, the innocent victim, so to speak? Well, yes and, oftentimes, no. Guilt is in the eye of the beholder.

Your spouse may be convinced that his or her cheating is a result of something you did or didn't do. Of course, in the majority of these situations, they may just be trying to justify their actions and avoid responsibility. But putting away your hurt feelings long enough to listen to your spouse is the only way you will be able to decide whether you should fight for the marriage or throw in the towel once and for all.

Exercise: Talking About Infidelity

When it comes to talking about infidelity, it is very easy for people to lose their heads and their tempers. But there can be no progress or healing until the couple launches an ongoing dialogue that will help them cope with the events and get on the road to reconciliation. The following are some good questions that can open up channels of communication.

1. What made you decide to stay in the relationship with me?

    _____

2. What qualities attracted you to the person you were having an affair with?

    _____

3. How did you feel lying to me about your whereabouts? Did you feel guilty or stressed?

_____

4. Did you think about what would happen if I found out? What did you think would be my response?

_____

5. What can I do to help you make a decision about the next step in our marriage?

_____

Reconciliation #2: Make a Firm Decision

Gerald, a 56-year-old ship owner, came to me after twenty-six years of being married to his wife, Priscilla. Gerald had fallen in love with her after hearing her sing at a New York jazz club. He quickly became smitten with her. Despite having come from an affluent family, Gerald didn't care who he married so long as he was in love.

Priscilla was the kind of woman who could never get used to being well off. You could tell by the way she clutched onto her Fendi bag for dear life that she was worried someone was going to take it away from her. Yet, the difference in their social status never mattered to the couple, and the pair were just glad to have found someone to share their lives with.

"For twenty-six years, Priscilla was the best wife you could ask for," Gerald conveyed. "Never late, good with the kids, always ready to help me with something. So when I found out that she was sleeping with our child's tutor, I was horrified. I never saw it coming. And my friends were just as horrified as I was. What made it so difficult was that in all the time we were married, we never once raised our voices to each other. My family and I were convinced that I was the luckiest man alive, and I vowed that I would try to be as good a husband as she was a wife.

"For a while, I almost didn't believe what had happened. We had a brief discussion during which she apologized and promised never to see him again. I told her I would think about it, but after five minutes I was the one begging for forgiveness. I couldn't imagine being without Priscilla.

"Three months went by and I never thought once about what had happened. But one night, I dreamt about Priscilla and the other man. Up until that point, I had never imagined them together. But once that door had been opened, there was no going back. I couldn't get the image of the two of them out of my mind. It was all I could think about. Another few months would go by before I'd finally decide that I could not forgive Priscilla for what she had done.

"I thought I could sweep what had happened under the rug, but I realized that it would not be that simple. I realized that I was still having a hard time deciding. I loved Priscilla very much, but I just couldn't get the image of them out of my head and that's why I wanted a divorce."

It seemed to me that Gerald would need more time to decide on what he was going to do. I knew he couldn't go on changing his mind forever. When I let him know that he needed to come back when he was comfortable with his final decision, he backed off right away.

You see, sometimes people come to me just because they want to see if they have what it takes to go through with the divorce. For some, it's almost like a test. Knowing full well that Gerald's indecision could last indefinitely, I suggested that he take some time to think about what he wanted and to stick with that no matter what. Gerald called me a week later to thank me for my time and to let me know that he would not be needing my services. He had decided to work things out with his wife.

The natural reaction of someone who's been cheated on is to vacillate between wanting to stay with their partner and needing to leave. From the stories I've heard, the most difficult act seems to be sticking to your resolution. Going back and forth, however, can be extremely damaging to the marriage, your partner, and yourself. If you find that you are unable to rise above your bitterness, do not try to make the marriage work. Your emotions will only manifest themselves in arguments and accusations. Once you've made a decision, you have to let your partner work to regain your trust despite your natural reservations. You have to take a leap of faith, and believe in your spouse's ability to be faithful. Otherwise, your spouse will never be able to rise above his or her past, and be the partner you want them to be.

On the other hand, if you decided to separate, make sure your decision is not a momentary reaction to an injustice. If your leaving is intended as some sort of revenge or grand gesture, then by all means drop the theatrics. Two people who are truly in love with one another can make an effort and right all wrongs by being honest and direct. Believe me, I've seen it happen.

Points to Ponder

1. Are there outside forces—family, friends, etc.—who are interfering with your relationship? If yes, have you considered asking them to give you time while you sort out the details?

   _____

2. Do you still love your spouse despite the infidelity?

   _____

3. Is there anything he or she can do to help you make your decision? If yes, have you expressed this to your spouse?

   _____

Reconciliation #3: Give Yourself Time

When Olivia, a 31-year-old pediatrician, came into my office, I could tell she was grappling with indecision. Her husband, Darren, a plastic surgeon, had cheated on her with a prostitute. Distraught and anxious about the future, she was still determined to save herself from what she was convinced was a damaging and destructive relationship.

"Darren was always around beautiful women, but I never worried that he would cheat on me because he always talked about how much he preferred natural and secure women such as myself to the neurotic ones who came into his office. Darren valued me for all of the things I valued in myself. I had always tried to support myself. I put myself through school and I never relied on anyone for help. Darren loved that about me, and always complimented me on being so self-sufficient.

"He liked the fact that I was smart and was never intimidated by it. For a long time, I was convinced that we were the perfect match. I couldn't have found anyone who understood me better.

"When Darren told me that he had been with a prostitute, I felt betrayed in more ways than I could ever say. I thought that he had been lying to me all along. Saying he admired strong, assertive women who could stand on their own two feet . . . if that was true, I thought, how could he ever be attracted to a prostitute? I became convinced that our entire relationship was built on lies and misrepresentation. I don't know Darren at all. And that's why I'm here."

After hearing Olivia discuss her marriage so favorably only to become so angry about her husband's affair, I knew that there was much more to the story than she was letting on. I knew that she was still in love with her husband, but uncertain as to what to do with the knowledge of his infidelity.

That's when I began asking her about Darren. She told me that he was torn up about her decision to get divorced and called every day to see how she was doing. She told me that he offered to seek counseling if only she would come back. It seemed that Olivia needed much more than a quick divorce; she needed someone who could help her make a decision. And although I knew there was hope for this couple, I wanted her to make a decision on her own. As I often do when a client is uncertain about filing for a divorce, I told her to come back and see me in a month. If she was still interested in getting a divorce, I would help her. But in the meantime, I recommended that she see a marital counselor with her husband.

As it turned out, Olivia and Darren got back together after six months of intensive therapy. Just as I had suspected, the couple had built a strong foundation, and were able to surmount the painful ordeal.

Time is one of the most powerful aids for someone who is grappling with infidelity. I cannot tell you how many relationships could have been salvaged if the couple had decided in favor of a trial separation, during which to think about the future of their marriage. Giving yourself time to come to grips with the pain of infidelity is the first step to surviving it. No one can be expected to make a rational decision when they are first confronted with their spouse's unfaithfulness. So if you're in doubt about whether to forgive or forget, accept your confusion until you are ready to make a decision that both you and your spouse can live with.

Infidelity: Closing Argument

Throughout the years, I have seen many couples come into my office ready to divorce on the grounds of infidelity. To most of them, it's an open and shut case—discover infidelity, get divorced. And although that may be the most appropriate solution for some couples, I can usually determine which couples are divorcing because they really wanted to and which filed for divorce to save face. You see, divorcing over infidelity is not an issue for your friends, family, or society to decide. I remember a client who had just gone through a terrible divorce, a divorce that hurt his children and his career. To add to his problems, he still loved his wife dearly. Obviously struggling, he looked at me and asked, "What could be worse than having your wife cheat on you?" The answer to that was suddenly clear to both of us—divorce.

In a great many cases, infidelity occurs when a spouse is frustrated in the marriage and does not feel capable of talking through his or her feelings. Infidelity often happens when the lines of communication break down. So in some cases, an affair can be a very misguided attempt to put a marriage back on track. I have been in many situations in which an affair actually led to improved communication and a stronger bond between a couple. For two people who love each other and are willing to do what it takes to make the relationship work, an affair does not have to signal the end. In fact, it's just the opposite; it could be the beginning of something much better.

TRANSITIONS

It would be nice to believe that all marriages that have stood the test of time have never dealt with a crisis or a major transition. It's easier to believe that those lucky couples have never had to cope with a death in the family or health problems, never renovated a home, never experienced financial setback like bankruptcy or unemployment, and never had to weather the empty-nest syndrome or a midlife crisis. But no matter how much we try to convince ourselves, there's no denying that crisis has a way of finding its way into everyone's life.

Even the happiest of couples have to deal with their share of problems and life stresses. You see, it's not how many crises befall a marriage, it's how a couple chooses to cope with that tragedy. From what I've seen (and believe me, I have pretty much seen it all) all marriages will eventually have to undergo extreme pressure under their weight of life's many burdens. But the couple's ability to lighten each other's load is what will ultimately determine the duration and strength of the marriage.

Jack, the general manager of a major sports team, was on the brink of divorce. Through mutual friends, I discovered that he had become extremely depressed. Now let me stress that this was one man who was always in the best of spirits. If anything, he could sometimes be a little too gregarious. A large, hulking man, he would shout out greetings, slap his friends on the back, and then proceed to crush their hands in what he tried to pass off as a handshake. He was quite a character.

His depression, however, was not something he was able to deal with successfully. It had been years since his father had passed away, and no matter what he did, he could not shake his grief. In fact, his suffering got worse with every passing day, until he could barely get out of bed.

His wife, Pauline, a drama coach at a prestigious university, had apparently had enough of his behavior. She had tried to be supportive in the beginning of the relationship, but, fearing that there would be no end to her husband's condition, she became concerned about fulfilling her own needs rather than constantly ministering to those of her husband.

"For a couple of months, I didn't think I was going to make it. But Pauline helped me stay afloat. She took time off work, made sure the kids were taken care of, and tried to engage me in conversation. Despite her efforts, I couldn't break out of the depression. I went on medication, and then went off when I experienced bad side effects. When the meds didn't work, Pauline became frustrated. She missed working full-time. I think she just had enough, and wanted to resume her old life."

Hearing Jack discuss the downward trajectory of his relationship saddened me considerably. I could tell that the couple had reached an impasse, and were struggling to surmount the crisis. Fortunately, their story came to a happy ending.

Pauline and Jack eventually got past the tough ordeal. Working with his psychologist, Jack was able to find a combination of medications that helped him get back on his feet and resume his old way of life. Pauline, too, began seeing a therapist in hopes of figuring out how best to cope with Jack's illness. What struck me most about their situation was how they managed to weather the storm, fighting to save their marriage even when it looked as though all hope was lost. Most important, their example started me thinking about the role of transitions in a marriage.

I began to wonder how other couples survived painful ordeals like health problems, death, and other painful disasters. I wondered: What did couples like Jack and Pauline know that others didn't? Watching them go through this terrible ordeal and come out stronger as a result, I knew there had to be a way of crisis-proofing a marriage, some kind of formula that happily married couples used to bounce back after major life setbacks. Whatever the secret, I was determined to figure it out.

Transition Assessment

You don't necessarily have to go through a big change or a major crisis to determine your level of adaptability. There are many questions that can help you assess whether you will be able to rise above life's challenges once the pressure is on. The following worksheet will give you a better understanding of how well you coped with transitions in the past and what you can do to improve your skills in the future.

1. Do you thrive on change or wish everything would stay as it was? Explain.

   _____

2. When starting a new job, are you usually apprehensive or excited about learning new things? Explain.

   _____

3. If you relocated, did you actively seek out new acquaintances or wait for others to approach you? Explain.

   _____

4. Has anyone close to you ever passed away? Explain how you dealt with that loss.

   _____

5. Have you ever been depressed? What led to the condition and what kind of treatment did you receive?

   _____

6. If something negative happened at work, would you tell your spouse about it or deal with it on your own? Explain.

_____

7. When faced with a financial worry, do you usually make a plan to fix the problem or spend many sleepless nights worrying about it? Explain.

_____

8. Do you believe in facing every problem head-on or do you prefer to wait and see what happens?

_____

9. Do you rely on your spouse to make major decisions about your home, children, and finances? Explain.

_____

Transitions: Warning Signs

Warning Sign #1: Obsessive Problem Solving

The knowledge that the world is not a perfect place, complete with neat solutions to complicated problems, is difficult for many of us to stomach. Our need to make sense out of our own lives, especially during very difficult times, can often cloud our thinking. When tragedy strikes, some people react by trying to fix the problem immediately. But what happens when there is no solution? Sometimes we must face the fact that we can't turn back the clock, and that the only solution is just being present as a source of solace and support for our loved ones when they need us most.

Jane, a 42-year-old publishing executive, was the victim of a violent attack. She was opening the door of her brownstone one night after a party, when a man approached her with a gun. He yelled at her to open the door. She did what he said, but before letting the door close behind her, began yelling and screaming at the top of her lungs. It was then that a man living across the street began screaming out of his apartment, threatening to come down and call the police. Seeing that there would be danger, the assailant tore Jane's pearl necklace off her neck and grabbed her wallet. He then fled the scene, and was never arrested by the police.

Jane's husband, Blake, had gone out of town for the weekend to visit his parents in Kansas City. When he called the next morning, he was greeted by a hysterical Jane, who could barely catch enough breath to tell him about what had happened the night before. Wanting to be by his wife's side, Blake caught the first flight into New York, and was home that same day.

"He accompanied me to the police station and helped me file all the reports. The police officer told me I was lucky, but I felt anything but. That night I had what would be the first of many sleepless nights. I began having the same nightmare over and over, and would wake up screaming in the middle of the night. Gradually, I also stopped going out of the house. For the first few days, I tried going to work, but I would freak out every time I saw someone who resembled the assailant. Fortunately, my company let me work part-time out of my house. Not that that helped me any. I became more isolated than ever. The only thing that kept me going was Blake. At first, I couldn't believe how concerned he was with my state of mind. He accompanied me to my counseling sessions, and would come during lunch to check up on me.

"What I didn't know was that Blake had got it into his head that he was responsible for what had happened. He was supposed to go to our friends' party with me, but decided to take advantage of a cheap weekend fare and visit his parents. What led to this discovery was his extreme behavior. When he saw I wasn't getting better, he became obsessed with finding out the identity of the attacker. He put up a million flyers warning local residents of the attacker, and offered a $5,000 reward to anyone who could help. I became more than a little concerned when he started organizing a neighborhood watch.

"He held weekly meetings at our house, and insisted that I cook something each time for the guests. He even stopped spending time with me. It seemed that he was either putting up flyers or scheduling meetings. All I wanted was his support and affection. I never wanted him to solve the problem. As if there was even a solution to be found. That was when I realized that his actions had very little to do with me, and everything to do with his own guilt for having gone out of town. I tried to explain that to him. But when I suggested that we should spend more time together, he lashed out at me, telling me that I was ungrateful and selfish. We started fighting a lot after that, and that's when I decided to file for a divorce. I couldn't think of any other options."

Judging by her manner and tone of voice, Jane was obviously desperate to figure out a solution to her marital problems. It was clear that she was still very much invested in the relationship, and that all she and Blake really needed was some time to sort through their problems. Blake was against the divorce from the beginning, but was unwilling to face up to his own guilt and role in the situation. Through conversations with both parties, we decided that it would be best to postpone the divorce proceedings until the couple spent some time in marriage counseling. Thanks to those sessions, Blake was able to accept what had happened, and found the comfort he needed to stop blaming himself for what happened to Jane. After that, it wasn't very hard for the couple to move on and begin their marriage with a renewed conviction of their deep love for one another.

Trying to fix a problem that has no solution is one way of dealing with a situation that is beyond our control. One of the most difficult aspects of dealing with a crisis is a lack of control, and many people will overcompensate for their feelings of insecurity. Difficulties can arise, however, when one partner is so consumed with getting their lives back on track that they lose sight of their partner's needs. Attempts to find a solution can be a proactive way of dealing with a problem, provided both partners are able to ban together to find a mutually satisfying resolution.

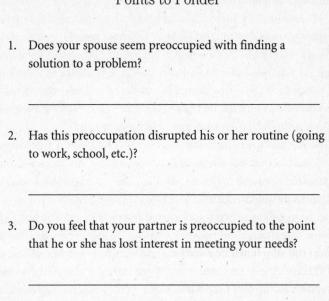

Points to Ponder

1. Does your spouse seem preoccupied with finding a solution to a problem?

   _____

2. Has this preoccupation disrupted his or her routine (going to work, school, etc.)?

   _____

3. Do you feel that your partner is preoccupied to the point that he or she has lost interest in meeting your needs?

   _____

Warning Sign #2: Denial of Problem

Dorian and Kelly had been married for ten years and had two children, Beth and Greg. They lived in a comfortable three-bedroom house in Connecticut, and enjoyed a relatively harmonious family life. Kelly stayed home with the children, while Dorian commuted to New York to work as the creative director of a national magazine. The couple had always assumed that they would enjoy the financial security they had become accustomed to. They were not wealthy, but always had enough to pay for their children's private school tuition and great holiday vacations.

"It came as a complete surprise when Dorian got laid off, at least to me. He came home and told me the news that same night when it happened. At first I tried to be supportive; after all, he was extremely talented and had a great reputation. I thought that it would only be a matter of time until he would be recruited to work at a better company, at a higher salary. I told him what I thought, and I'll never forget how he looked at me. His face turned ashen white and his eyes were cloudy. He said, in a very strange voice, 'Nothing will ever be the same again.'

"I tried to laugh it off, but then he told me what had really happened. He explained that he had been working freelance at a competitive magazine for over two years. He was found out, and the word had leaked out about him all over town. He wouldn't be getting a job anytime soon, not in New York or anywhere for that matter."

"Well, I don't have to tell you how shocked I was. I immediately started looking over our financial situation. I called my parents and his parents for help as well. Dorian, on the other hand, stopped working altogether. He quietly put all his belongings away, and walked around the house in a daze. When the kids tried to talk with him, he was unresponsive and elusive. They asked him why he was home, and he told them he had simply stopped working and would never work again."

"When I tried to talk to him about our financial situation, he would refuse, demanding that I leave him alone. Seeing that our reserve funds were not going to last us too long, I decided to get a job, but even that became a big hassle. Dorian didn't understand why I needed to work. Meanwhile, money was getting tighter every passing day.

"One day I looked at him and just started yelling. I told him that he was watching our lives go down the drain, and that he refused to do anything to help. He wouldn't look for a new job, and was in complete denial about the state of our finances. I just couldn't take it anymore. I could accept that he couldn't deal with what was happening around him at that time, but to try and prevent me from taking charge? Now, that I couldn't deal with."

My heart went out to both Dorian and Kelly. I could imagine how hard it must have been on Dorian to go from being on top of the world to being disgraced in front of his peers and family. And although I didn't condone his business practices, I felt extremely sorry for him and Kelly. Nobody explains how to deal with these kinds of problems before marriage, and the couple had no idea how to get themselves out of this mess.

I talked to Kelly at length about her relationship with Dorian and his future. She told me that he had begun toying with the idea of going to law school, but was unable to get motivated. She let me know that they had discussed a trial separation, and I encouraged her to give it a shot before making the decision to divorce. It seemed to me that Dorian had grown to rely on Kelly too much, and that being alone might be just what he needed to get out of his predicament.

It turned out that my instincts were right. Without Kelly there to worry about the family and generally pick up the slack, Dorian began to feel responsible for the children's welfare. Propelled by his newfound self-sufficiency, he began looking for temporary work while applying to graduate school.

One of the biggest difficulties all of us face is change. There is no telling how a person will react to a new development or a stressful life change. While some people are able to face the problem head-on, others tend to deny the events, hoping that their lives will magically return to normal. Denial may be one of our most enduring survival traits, but in the end, it is those people who are able to adapt to the life transitions who will have the easiest time.

The same goes for couples. One person may try to avoid thinking about the situation, while the other insists on confronting the issues. As you can imagine, couples with different styles of coping can either be of great assistance to one another or can experience conflict when trying to resolve the life crisis. The key is for both people to remain flexible, and try to look at the situation from both their own and their partner's perspective.

Points to Ponder

1. Does your spouse think you're not interested in helping to solve family problems?

2. When last faced with a challenge, did you consistently try
    to shift responsibility to your spouse?

    _____

3. Do you prefer to solve problems as they arise or wait to see
    if they will go away on their own? How does your spouse
    react in similar situations?

    _____

Warning Sign #3: Emotional Withdrawal

Ronald, a respected speech writer and political consultant, had filed for
a divorce from his wife, Sarah, of ten years. Ronald and Sarah had
resided on the Upper East Side in a well-appointed, two-bedroom
condo. Sarah was a 35-year-old doctor with her own medical practice.
The couple never had any children, but were content because of their
busy careers and good relationship.

The trouble began when Sarah's father was diagnosed with lung
cancer. The two of them were very close, always talking on the phone
and sending letters. The diagnosis hit Sarah's family very hard, considering that he was planning to retire that year. Given only one month to
live, Sarah's father wanted all of his family around him, and Sarah
immediately flew home to Ohio to be by his side.

"I was there for Sarah in every way possible. I even offered to fly down
with her. But because her father never liked me—he thought I was too old
for her—she thought it would be best if I didn't go. Still, I wanted to see her
and be there for her. So I decided to surprise her. When I arrived, I could
barely get one minute alone with her. Someone was always needing her
help. Sarah told me point-blank that I shouldn't have come. She was angry
with me for defying her, and felt that I didn't respect her wishes. On the
contrary, I just wanted to show her how much I loved her.

"At first, I was hurt when she told me to leave. But I decided to put my feelings on hold. She was the one suffering, and I wasn't about to make it any worse. I left the next day. To my surprise, Sarah didn't call me for weeks. I was very nervous about what was happening to her. I called and called, but her mother said she didn't want to be disturbed.

"Finally, one night at three o'clock in the morning, I received a phone call. It was Sarah. I was so excited to hear her voice, I almost fell out of bed. But the phone call made me more distressed than ever. Sarah's father had passed away a week ago. I told her I loved her and that I was sorry for her loss. Thinking that she would be flying home, I asked her when I should expect her. That's when she told me that she would not be home for another month. Her mother needed someone by her side, and Sarah didn't want to leave her.

"I tried to convince her to bring her mother to New York. We had the extra bedroom, but she wouldn't hear of it. When I asked her if I could visit her, she became annoyed with me and told me that I should just leave her alone; that I had no idea what she was going through. This was all very strange, because Sarah was always very affectionate with me in the past. Her tone was so cold and callous. It was like talking to another person.

"Still, I hoped she would be back to her old ways once she had time to adjust. A month went by. She only called twice to give me some help with household things. Six weeks later I hadn't heard from her, and decided that I would have to go to Ohio to straighten things out. But when I got there, she couldn't even look at me. I tried to hug her, but she cringed and turned away. I was lost. I didn't know what to do. I demanded that she come home, and she, of course, yelled back at me, telling me that she hated me and never wanted to see me again. I told her that if she didn't come home immediately, I would divorce her. And that was it . . . I flew back home and we've barely talked since."

Ronald had come to me to get a divorce, but I could see that he still had hope for the marriage. His threats of divorce were little more than a frustrated man's last-ditch efforts to get his wife back. Of course, this only pushed Sarah further away.

As with all my clients, I let Ronald know that his actions would have irrevocable consequences. There would be no going back. I suggested that he leave a window of opportunity open for Sarah's return. After getting Ronald to see that both he and Sarah were frustrated with the added pressure and were acting out as a result, I talked him into postponing the divorce proceedings until he'd exhausted every possibility for reconciliation.

A few months later, the situation had simmered down and Robert called me to let me know that Sarah would be arriving at LaGuardia airport that night. I could tell he was very relieved, even if he acted like he'd known that cooler heads would prevail all along.

A crisis can not only change the way we feel about the world; it can change the way we feel about our marriage. It is not at all uncommon in the wake of a tragedy to feel detached from your spouse, especially if your spouse isn't going through the same difficulties that you are. Anger also plays a significant factor. Not only is the person under significant stress having to deal with their own private rage, but your presence serves as a constant reminder that you are not experiencing the same amount of pain. And although your spouse should be happy that you are absolved from their troubles, they are more likely to resent that fact.

Points to Ponder

1. Has your spouse stopped seeking you out for emotional support? If yes, are you hurt by their inability to confide in you?

   _____

2. Have you ever felt that you couldn't rely on your partner to help you during a crisis? Please explain.

   _____

3. Does your spouse experience feelings of isolation and depression? If yes, do you try to give him or her space to work out their problem?

Transitions: Crimes and Misdemeanors

Crime and Misdemeanor #1: Laying Blame

Working together to solve a major crisis is one of the fundamental factors contributing to a lasting marriage. The most destructive thing anyone can do is turn this principle on its head. And yet that is precisely what we do when we blame our spouses for our marital problems—we pit ourselves against our spouses and wind up trying to defeat instead of help one another. Even if the crisis was in large part due to someone's negligence, pointing out those facts will only make an unstable situation that much more precarious.

Danny, a deli owner, came to see me about getting a divorce from Helen, his wife of thirty years. Although the fire had gone out many years ago, the couple respected and understood each other. As Danny explained, leaving his wife had never been an option, but in light of recent events, he saw no other way.

"It happened so quickly. It was Sunday afternoon and I had closed up shop early to come home in time for my Sunday night poker game with some of my buddies. Helen was visiting a friend nearby and wouldn't be home for a few hours. I had just begun to get my dinner ready when the phone rang. It was the police. They were calling to tell me that there was a fire at the store and I should come down immediately.

"When I got there, it looked like the whole place was engulfed by flames. There were fire trucks everywhere and it was obvious that there was going to be some serious damage. Although I had insurance, the store was my whole life, and it was terrible to have to stand there and watch it burn to the ground.

"Helen arrived on the scene soon after. She looked even more panic-stricken than I was. Once the fire was extinguished, the police began their investigation. It turns out that I had left a small oven on by mistake. I felt terrible. I couldn't believe what I had done. And I didn't even know when I would get the insurance money because of the investigation.

"For weeks, I was in shock. I walked around trying to figure out what had happened, but I simply couldn't wrap my mind around it. Helen was also acting stranger and stranger with every passing day. She began by asking me what I planned to do next. Gradually, her nagging escalated into outright blaming me for ruining both our lives.

"I was feeling very guilty as it was, and the last thing I needed was to have Helen blame me for what happened. Not only that, but I began to feel worse and worse, thinking about all the things I could have done differently, until I could barely stand to be with myself.

"Finally, I had had enough. I had to do something for myself. I was stressed and angry all the time. The guilt I was feeling was beginning to take over my life, and I had to get out of the marriage to save what was left of my self-respect."

When a couple finds themselves faced with a major crisis, it is very tempting to look for a scapegoat. Trying to make sense of a random accident can be very destructive to marital well-being. Invariably, one partner feels the weight of responsibility leveled on their shoulders, which can be the beginning of the end for the relationship. Not only that, but laying blame can make each partner feel like they are on opposite sides versus on the same team, which is critical to future happiness and peaceful coexistence.

Points to Ponder

1. Do you believe your spouse was somehow responsible for your predicament? If yes, please explain.

2. Have you vocalized this belief? If yes, how did your partner respond to your claims?

    _____

3. What factors, other than your spouse's actions, could have contributed to the crisis or transition? List as many as applicable.

    _____

Crime and Misdemeanor #2:
Coddling Your Spouse

Geraldine and Barry had been married for only one year when she was hit by a car crossing Fifth Avenue. The accident left her severely impaired, but the doctors promised that with regular physical therapy, she would have a full recovery. Still, she had to take a year's leave of absence from her high-ranking position at a large architectural firm in Manhattan, something she was very upset about. Barry, a young art dealer, was naturally relieved to find that his wife would recover. He was making enough money to support both of them, and had never wanted his wife to work in the first place. From what Geraldine told me, it sounded as if Barry was actually happy to have his wife at home.

"When I got home from the hospital, I found Barry in the best of spirits. He even planned a small surprise party for me to commemorate my homecoming. After the party, he took me to my room, where he showed me all of the special devices and gadgets he had built in. There was a bell for when I needed something, a magazine rack full of magazines, and a list of emergency numbers written in large print taped to my nightstand. The one thing that was missing was my drafting table. When I asked him where it was, he told me he moved it out so I would have more room to move around in my wheelchair.

"I didn't think twice about it. I was actually relieved that he loved me enough to accept me in any condition. But gradually, Barry's concern began to work against me. Barry was always calling home to see how I was doing. He also started ordering my meals for me without asking what I wanted. When I complained, he just laughed and told me that he didn't want me straining myself. When he came home, he would drop all of his activities just to be with me. If anything, I wanted to have some time to myself, to think about what had happened and how I was going to get my life back. But Barry was determined not to leave me alone for one minute.

"It got to the point that I began looking forward to my painful physical therapy sessions. It was the only time when I could be without Barry. I was doing really well, too, until Barry began insisting that he come in with me when I complained how much strain my muscles were under. He became convinced that my therapist was working me too hard, and wouldn't leave despite my asking him to. Two months later, my doctor called me to tell me that he wasn't pleased with my rate of recovery. He had expected me to be doing much better. I felt ashamed, like I let everyone down. Most of all, I felt helpless and unable to control my life.

"What really got me thinking about Barry's role in my condition was his lack of interest in my recovery. He was never late for anything, but he began showing up late to drive me to physical therapy. One time he didn't show up at all, and I couldn't track him down for hours. I let it slide the first time, but when it happened the second time, I became angry. What really put me over the edge is when Barry came home one day with a nurse. He told me that she would be taking care of me. But I didn't need a nurse, I just needed some help getting back on my feet. It was clear to me at that point that Barry was more interested in taking care of me than helping me take care of myself. I understood then that if I ever hoped to recover I would have to get out of what seemed to be a destructive relationship."

I've seen this kind of excessive concern, where a spouse uses a life transition as a way of taking control of their spouse, in many marriages. In Geraldine's and Barry's case, Barry was all too happy to have his wife at home. He had always resented the job that took Geraldine away from him, and saw the opportunity as a chance to get control of a situation in which he felt helpless.

Using kindness as a disguise for trying to get control of a situation or a person was what ultimately brought my client Jerry to the brink of divorce. Jerry's high-stress job as a homicide detective eventually caught up with him when he suffered a nervous breakdown, and was instructed to take a leave of absence from work.

His wife, Sylvia, who had always feared for Jerry's safety, was all too happy to have him at home and to minister to his every need. In fact, she was so relieved to have her husband out of harm's way that she was determined to keep him by her side forever by making sure he was well taken care of. All Jerry had to do was think about something, whether it was a glass of water or a new book, and it would magically appear. For a while he had the best of both worlds until he realized how spoiled he had become by Sylvia's attentions. He even asked for more autonomy only to be ignored by his wife. What had started as a temporary leave of absence turned into a long two-year break.

Feelings of helplessness; feelings of being unable to surmount an obstacle; almost guarantee that you won't. A sense of self-sufficiency is not the natural reaction to a crisis. Most people feel anything but capable of handling their own problems during a crisis. It's hard enough dealing with life's many challenges without having your spouse make you feel like a victim. The best gift anyone could give someone who's going through a tough time is the gift of empowerment. And there is nothing more empowering than feeling that you can solve problems on your own.

Points to Ponder

1. Do you ever feel that your spouse's concern is excessive, causing you to depend on him or her?

_____

2. Do you wish your spouse would help you help yourself instead of trying to fix everything him- or herself?

   _____

3. Have you ever been guilty of trying to do too much for your spouse out of feelings of obligation or out of a desire to protect him or her?

   _____

Crime and Misdemeanor #3: Lashing Out

Lauren, a 35-year-old film producer, came to me to file for a divorce from her husband of three years, Larry. She was a feisty, no-holds-barred kind of woman, whose cell phone was always on. She didn't have a stitch of makeup on, and was wearing an expensive man-tailored suit. I was surprised we even got through the first meeting, considering how many phone calls she took during that hour.

"It was doomed from the beginning. We met while working on a big summer film. He was a good director, I have to hand him that. I liked him right away, even though he was much older. Our first argument, though, really clinched it for me. He was so combative, not giving an inch. So I asked him out to dinner. I should have known that what began with a fight would end the same way. We got married not much later. Everything was good. I had a string of hits under my belt that year, and Larry was also working like a madman. We were probably both at the peak of our careers. That could have been why we didn't have any problems.

"That all changed when Larry was taken off a picture. He had gotten into a fight with one of the producers, and was labeled a 'loose cannon.'

Nobody wanted to work with him. His career was going down fast. I've never been the sensitive type, but I really felt bad. It wasn't fair what happened to him. Larry took it hard. He was angry with the system and himself. He was also angry with me. I was still going off to work each day, while he stayed home sulking. I could tell that his male ego was hurt by the way he scowled at me whenever I talked about work.

"I was really in a bind. On the one hand, I wanted to help him; on the other I was worried that he would turn me away. He always had a hard time accepting suggestions from me. One day I got in touch with a friend's agent and asked him to pull some strings for me. There was a new movie that I thought Larry would be perfect for, and I wanted him to get the job. When he got the call, he was thrilled. I had never seen him so happy. He was screaming and carrying on like a two-year-old. I was just happy I could do something for him, and hoped he wouldn't find out about what I did.

"Somehow, a few months later, the mutual friend whose agent I used to get Larry the job, told my husband what happened. The first I heard about it was when Larry called me on the set. He started cursing me out and yelling at me, like how could I humiliate him like that. Seeing that he was in an irrational mood, I hung up the phone. I came home that night and found all of my things tossed in the hall. My clothes were slashed, and all of my belongings broken into tiny pieces. I was so angry, I even called the police. I knew he had problems, but I couldn't believe he was capable of doing that."

Extreme stress can make people do funny things. It can cause forgetfulness, compulsive reactions, and a myriad of other reactions that can be classified as "crazy." A little bit of insanity is expected of people faced with what seem at the time to be insurmountable obstacles. But verbal and physical abuse should never be tolerated or justified, even in the most extreme situations. No matter how hard a time a person is having, there is absolutely no excuse for losing your temper. People sometimes feel that if they make someone feel worse, they will feel better. But if that's someone's main coping strategy, you can be certain it will resolve nothing, and will only create more difficulties down the line.

Points to Ponder

1. Have you ever acted irrationally during times of stress?

   _____

2. Have you ever wanted to inflict physical harm or hurt yourself while going through a personal crisis?

   _____

3. Do you fear your spouse becoming stressed for fear of what he or she will do?

   _____

Crime and Misdemeanor #4:
Making Unreasonable Demands

Harvey, a marketing director for a large dot-com, was convinced that his wife, Janine, a self-employed business consultant, was trying to sabotage his career. Although he had a mild-mannered air, I could tell that Harvey could only be pushed so far, and what he told me next confirmed that suspicion.

"Janine was always a very aggressive businesswoman. It served her well most of the time, but not always. It was her attitude problem that finally alienated her key client, a national magazine. When she lost that account, she was devastated. She tried everything, going after the client's competitors and bad-mouthing them to other companies. That only aggravated the situation, and other clients soon fell by the wayside. Her business was going through a major crisis. That's when she asked—I should say demanded—that I get her a job at my company. I wanted to help her, and knew she needed to save face in front of her ex-clients. And despite having major reservations about mixing business and my personal life, I set about and was successful at finding her a position at my company. When she got to the company, she was very cooperative of everyone there. It was great at first. We would go out to lunch and talk during our downtimes. But things changed when she began having problems with a valued coworker. I had worked with this man for over ten years. I hired him myself. I had never found him difficult to work with, so was very surprised that he and my wife were having a personality conflict. All the while I hoped things would work out on their own.

"One day my wife stormed into my office and demanded that I fire her adversary. Well, I couldn't believe what I was hearing. Not only was he a very competent employee, he had a wife and two children to support. I couldn't very well fire him just to please my wife. When I refused to comply with her demands, she became belligerent, accusing me of favoring him over her. But no matter how much I tried to defend myself, I came off looking like the bad guy, like the kind of husband who doesn't love his wife enough to defend her. After two weeks of back and forth and trying to work out the hostile work environment, Janine laid down an ultimatum. It was either her or my old colleague. At that point, I was so aggravated that I picked the latter. There was nothing I could do. She was being completely unreasonable. I knew that if I gave in to her then, my whole life with her would become a no-win situation."

In their effort to survive a crisis, some people have a tendency to go into combat mode. They want to battle the negative circumstances by any means possible, which can often lead to extremist thinking. Despite having the best intentions, people in combat mode will often make unreasonable demands on their partner, asking them to do things they would never do, like relocate, find unsuitable jobs, or fire their best employees. For them, trying to get control over their spouse is merely an attempt to get control over their chaotic lives. So if you find yourself demanding something of your spouse that you would never demand of yourself, try letting go of the things you can't control.

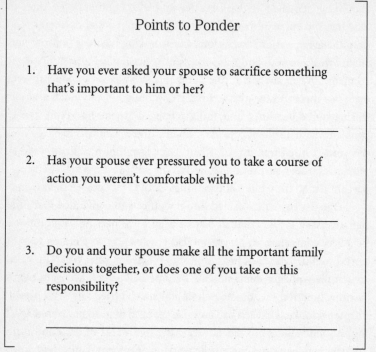

Points to Ponder

1. Have you ever asked your spouse to sacrifice something that's important to him or her?

   _____

2. Has your spouse ever pressured you to take a course of action you weren't comfortable with?

   _____

3. Do you and your spouse make all the important family decisions together, or does one of you take on this responsibility?

   _____

Transitions: Effecting a Reconciliation

Reconciliation #1: Stay Flexible

Theresa and Peter had been married for twenty years. The couple resided in a spacious apartment on the Upper East Side. They were reasonably well off. Theresa ran her own full-service salon, and he was a Wall Street broker. When Theresa came to see me it was after having gone through one of the most difficult rites of passage any marriage can go through—remodeling.

"My business was doing fairly well, and I don't have to tell you that everyone was making out well in the market. So after reviewing all our finances, we decided that we could finally afford to renovate our two-bedroom apartment. It would be a big job. Everything from the kitchen to the bathrooms would have to be completely redone. There would be shopping to do, design decisions to make. It was a project I had wanted to start for so long that I threw myself into it completely. Peter was also very involved from the beginning. He helped me set a budget, assisted in interviewing the designers, and even negotiated with the contractors I chose.

"We also found out that if we wanted to really redo the entire apartment, we couldn't afford to move out to a hotel. With the prices being what they are, we really would not have enough to accomplish everything we wanted to. So we made a decision to do one room at a time, that way we could relocate each time we began renovating a new area. The idea seemed perfectly reasonable then, but it turned out to be the worst decision we ever made. Our decision slowed down the process significantly. The workers could not work as fast with us and all of our stuff being in their way.

"I remember coming home tired after work, and there would be all this rubble on the floor—spilled paint, tools, wood shavings. It was a mess. But still we would have to put up with it. I tried to stay positive throughout the ordeal, but every passing day saw me and Peter become more impatient with the process and each other. Soon we were picking fights with one another about the smallest things. I remember a row we had about the paint; he wanted bone white and I wanted ivory white. Looking back now, the difference was so minimal, but it meant so much back then.

"As the months progressed and the contractors were no closer to finishing the job, we began to lose it. We just didn't feel comfortable in our own home. The chaos there began to seep into our minds, until we were barely able to get up to go to work each day. When six months passed, I knew we had to do something to save not only our marriage but our minds. I told Peter that we would have to move out to a hotel. But he wouldn't listen. He kept yelling about the fact that we had made a decision and we would stick to it, like somehow his pride was on the line and he wouldn't second-guess himself. I asked him to do it for us. At that point, I honestly didn't think we would make it. Yet he still wouldn't budge. It would be another three months until our apartment was looking perfect. Unfortunately, we had decided to divorce and would not be living there long enough to enjoy it."

This is just one of the many cases in which a major home redo has led to marital dissolution. I had another case, almost ten years ago, in which something similar happened. Jordan, a young teacher and social worker, and her husband Ron, a sales manager, had always had to scrimp and save. Finally, after years of saving they had enough money to redecorate. Unfortunately, they hired the wrong contractor, and were soon in a difficult position. They didn't have enough money to finish the job and had to live in worse conditions than when they started. The paint was chipping, the floors were stripped bare. The haphazard conditions had finally gotten to them, and they began fighting with one another.

Thankfully, before they decided to proceed with the divorce, the couple made one last-ditch effort to salvage their marriage. Through some friends who were stationed overseas, they were able to secure temporary housing in the south of France. In the end, what could have turned into a nightmarish divorce became a pleasant second honeymoon. Because Jordan and Ron stayed flexible in times of trouble and found a creative solution, the couple was able to adapt to their circumstances and even derive some pleasure from a negative situation.

Every major life transition and crisis requires us to adapt to a new way of living, a whole new set of circumstances that we are rarely ready to face. But let me remind you that divorce is more a tragic consequence than an easy fix. Instead of making separation the foregone conclusion, I implore you to make every attempt to adapt to your new situation. Sometimes taking a break can be all it takes to weather one of life's storms; sometimes it can mean trying out several different approaches to the same problem. Being able to make decisions that will help you better cope with the situation requires a certain amount of flexibility. Tempting as it is to hold on to the past with all our might during troubling times, it is actually the worst thing we can do for ourselves and our marriage.

Exercise: Flexibility Assessment

Please answer True or False to the following statements.

1. Once I find a solution, I stick to it no matter what happens.
    True _____ False _____

2. I have a hard time changing my mind.
   True _____ False _____

3. People sometimes call me demanding and controlling.
   True _____ False _____

4. I have a hard time adjusting to new people and places.
   True _____ False _____

If you replied "True" to more than two of the above statements, you'll have to make a concerted effort to think about all of the possible options available to you. To help yourself stay flexible, ask your partner or a trusted friend to list all the possible solutions to your problem. Don't make the mistake of choosing a solution immediately. Take the time to mull over each scenario and give some serious thought to how it can benefit you in the long run.

Reconciliation #2: Work Together

The most important factor determining whether a couple will bounce back from adversity or crumble beneath its weight is their ability to band together in times of trouble. When crisis strikes, it's all too easy to focus on selfish needs and desires. After all, most people like to feel as if they deserve some time to grieve and act out. And they do. But what often happens is that while one person is going through a selfish period, the other is left alone to pick up the pieces and restore order. This may be natural, but it can also cause resentment when one person continually takes on the role of the rock and the other that of victim. It's very important to be able to switch roles once in a while to give your partner some space to breathe and collect themselves. Think of this as being on the same team in a tug of war; there's a time to pick up the slack and a time to ease up.

Ron, a bank manager from Long Island, had come into my office to discuss getting a divorce from his wife of twenty years, Wendy.

"When the kids left for school, I knew that there would be some loneliness. Maybe the house would be quiet. Maybe we'd have more free time on our hands. I didn't know what would happen, but I knew things would be different. Wendy and I were always consumed by the kids' lives—we have a boy, Tommy, and a girl, Elizabeth. Before they left for school, I tried to talk to Wendy about how our lives would change. I tried to come up with some ideas for us—joining clubs, picking up new hobbies, those kinds of things. But Wendy wouldn't participate.

"She thought I was having a crisis, but I knew that we both needed to find some new ways to occupy our time. Still, she didn't try to meet me halfway, even after she became depressed and down. She missed the kids terribly, and didn't want to do anything with me. After work, she would come home, check her e-mail to see if the kids had written, and go to bed to watch TV. When I tried to talk to her and suggest outings and activities, she shunned me and told me that I should leave her alone. It's not as if I was trying only for her. I also missed the kids, and needed some help and her companionship. When I didn't get it, I decided it was time to do something. I don't know if divorce is the solution, but I do know something has to change."

Ron left my office more dejected than ever. He was clearly not ready for a divorce, but he wanted to make sure Wendy was aware of his frustration. A few weeks later, Ron called to tell me that his wife was extremely distraught by the idea of a divorce and they had gone to their local priest to try to work it out. Slowly, Wendy came to take her responsibility for the marriage more seriously, and worked in tandem with Ron to make the adjustment from a full to an empty nest.

The empty-nest syndrome can prove to be a difficult transition for couples who haven't prepared adequately. And Ron and Wendy's story was proof of that. But what Ron's story also revealed to me was just how deeply their lives had become intertwined and how much they would need each other to make it through life's many storms. The problem was that Ron was doing all the work. Wendy, meanwhile, had grown so accustomed to Ron taking charge that she completely lost sight of her own responsibility. Ron's situation was just as depressing as her own, and he needed her support as much as she needed his. This is a classic example of two people who have the same goals, but for one reason or another cannot find the common ground needed to work through their ordeal as a team.

What you have to remember is that no matter what your spouse is saying and doing, no matter how many times they tell you to leave them alone, or even turn on you for making a serious mistake, never take their words to heart and try to be there for each other in every way possible during the crisis.

Exercise: Helping a Partner in Crisis

1. Don't think about how your partner's behavior reflects on you.

2. Try to be as objective as possible. Treat your spouse as you would a dear and valued friend.

3. Try not to think about what *you* would do in the same situation. Focus on what's best for your spouse.

4. Empower your spouse to make decisions for him- or herself.

5. Set guidelines and deadlines for making important decisions.

6. Show your partner how supportive you are by listening and being understanding.

Resolution #3: Making Temporary Sacrifices

Nina, a successful European model, wanted my services in divorcing her husband, Jason, of four years. Her modeling career had been going strong since she was seventeen years old and won a prestigious modeling competition, but only recently had she decided to branch out into acting. It was a decision she had been grappling with for years. Nina met Jason, a PR director, while working on a publicity campaign for a large shoe manufacturer. Jason had launched a new campaign, which Nina was working on as well. The couple had an instant attraction, and married soon after.

"Modeling always made things difficult between us. There was the traveling and constant rivalries. At first, Jason was a little jealous. That was only natural. I had to do the entire party circuit and meet a lot of influential and important men. But he knew I loved him. He was right. I met the most exciting and brilliant men from all over the world, but all I could think about was coming home to Jason.

"After three years, I thought we would be together forever. Jason always encouraged me to challenge myself. And I decided to take acting classes in New York for several months. My agency was convinced that I could really make a name for myself, and was sending me out on auditions for movies and television films. It was very exciting to try something new. But it wasn't always fun. I wasn't very good at the auditions at first and I wasn't getting any jobs. My agency told me to have patience. Finally, a movie director called and asked me to star in a new movie. It didn't have a very big budget, but it was a good start. The only problem was that it was a very sexy film. They wanted me to appear naked. They wouldn't negotiate.

"I wanted to make the right decision, so I asked Jason what he thought. He read the script and, to my surprise, forbade me to do it. He said it would ruin my career, that I would make a disgrace out of both of us. He said it was only a step above pornography. But I didn't agree with him. I worked very hard to get where I was. I wanted to become an actress, and this seemed to be the only way. Jason just didn't get it.

"When I told him I was doing it, he refused to talk to me for weeks. I told him that this was a one-time thing, that I needed to get my feet wet. I begged him to be understanding. But he wouldn't budge. He wouldn't listen. The shoot lasted for only two months. It was hard enough for me trying to learn to act and starting a new career. He didn't do anything to help. All he had to do was congratulate me, or even just be quiet about how much he hated the movie, but he didn't do either. When I finished the movie, I got better roles. But by that time Jason and I were considering moving out into separate apartments."

At the time, Nina and Jason had not had the benefit of marital counseling. Devastated by Jason's inability to support her career and her decisions, Nina had been trying to get Jason into couples counseling for months with no success. A week after she came in to see me, though, Nina called and told me that Jason was making an effort to see what had happened from her point of view. His behavior probably came about as the result of Nina's visit to my office. Once he realized just how close he'd come to losing his wife, Jason decided to take action.

Although not all of my clients' stories end well, this one did because Jason finally saw how foolish and uncaring he had been. Scared by the possibility that Nina would become a huge star and abandon him, Jason had become hostile and resentful. Once he worked through some of his concerns with a therapist, the couple was able to rebound and renew their commitment to one another.

Making sacrifices is a marital inevitability. There are times when we have to put aside our ideas, values, and routines in order to save the relationship. And never is that more true than during a time of transition. Transitions have a tendency to make all of us feel vulnerable and unsure about our future prospects, and those emotions can make people cling to what they know and become rigid and inflexible. They are so consumed by the prospect of giving up their way of life, that they often forget about what their partner's needs are and how to meet those needs. I know because I've seen people try to cope with the toughest transition of all—divorce.

You must understand that compromising will not affect the rest of your life or how you feel about yourself. It is not an issue of pride or ego. Many times sacrifices, like moving to a new town or quitting a job, have to be made to further the common objective of keeping your marriage intact.

Exercise: Compromise Worksheet

Reaching a compromise with your spouse is easier said than done. It always seems that one partner feels that he or she has given up more than the other. More important, he or she often feels that their sacrifices have gone unappreciated. This lack of acknowledgment makes the sting of giving up what they want that much harder to bear. To remedy this situation, consider keeping track of who's giving up what. Of course, your marriage should not be about keeping score or a running tally. But if this is what it takes to understand that both of you are giving an inch, then keeping count is worth a try.

Issue #1:

_____

Spouse's Solution

_____

_____

Your Solution

_____

_____

Compromise

_____

_____

_____

Issue #2:

_____

Spouse's Solution

_____

_____

Your Solution

_____

_____

Compromise

_____

_____

Reconciliation #4: Find Time for Play

Tracy and Ashton had been married for three years. Tracy, an attractive and well-put-together marketing writer, wanted to file for a divorce from her husband, who worked as a director of business development for an on-line start-up. The transition that sparked their decision to separate was Ashton's prostate cancer. He had always tried hard to stay in shape and eat healthy, so when he received the diagnosis, he and Tracy were understandably terrified by the situation.

"I couldn't believe it. Ashton was only 44 years old. When we first found out, it was like our lives stopped, like everything we had planned for—moving out of our old apartment, flying to Italy, Ashton's promotion—was suddenly put on hold. Frankly, we had never dealt with anything like that before. We were unprepared for what would come next.

"At first, we decided that we would do everything to get Ashton well. We went to the best specialists and read every book we could find about prostate cancer. As you can imagine, it wasn't fun. If anything, we were making ourselves, each other, and our daughter, Shela, completely stressed. When I heard that her grades in school were slipping, I knew that we were somehow responsible for her lack of motivation. Our household was grim. I don't think anyone had smiled for months.

"That's when I became determined to save not only Ashton but our marriage and family. I knew that being anxious or worried would not help anyone. If anything, our doctor told me that Ashton would feel better once he learned to accept his diagnosis and make the best of the situation. So one day, at dinner, I looked around at Ashton's and Shela's dour expressions, and decided to have some fun. I threw some food at them, hoping to start a food fight. Shela joined right in, and threw some back. But Ashton just looked at me disapprovingly and left the table. His reaction was devastating, but I knew that I shouldn't give up.

"For several months, I tried everything I could to cheer him up. I invited him to see funny movies . . . nothing. Not even a smile. I arranged for us to go dancing, and even threw some parties with our closest friends . . . nothing. There was nothing I could do. Ashton was determined to be unhappy."

Tracy was obviously distraught over her husband's condition and what it was doing to her family. She had fought very hard to maintain their life together, but I could see that she would need her husband's full cooperation if the marriage was to survive. After we began the process of filing for divorce, Tracy came to me and asked me to hold off for a little while.

Thanks to Tracy's ceaseless efforts to lighten the family's mood, Ashton was finally beginning to come around and enjoy life again. Tracy wasn't sure if his improved mood would last, but she certainly didn't want to ruin their chances by giving up too soon. That Christmas, I received a phone call from Tracy, letting me know that Ashton's illness was in remission and they were meeting with a therapist regularly to keep the marriage on track.

There are many people who wonder how anyone going through a life crisis can find the will to have fun or distract themselves. After all, how could we possibly deal with our problem if we're not constantly worrying and thinking about it? Although facing things head-on has its time and place, distraction and amusement is one of the most effective ways of boosting your spirits and overcoming your difficulties.

It is clear that the people who overcome life stresses are the ones who are able to find lighthearted distractions to occupy their time. They are able to put their dilemma in a larger framework, and find the perspective they need to weather the transition. The problem comes in when one partner mistakes the other's lightheartedness for disinterest or lack of affection. Some people assume that if their partner doesn't brood as much as they do, that they somehow care less. Although that may be an easy assumption to make, it is usually a false one. So if you find your spouse trying to distract you from your troubles, don't take their behavior as a dismissal of your problem's importance, but as a confirmation of their deep love for you.

Transitions: Closing Argument

For all our planning, life has a tendency to throw us one curveball after another. Things can go smoothly for years and years. And then, just when you think it's safe to relax and enjoy yourself, your whole life can change drastically in the time it takes for me to snap my fingers. There are some events for which we just can't prepare, no matter how hard we try. The loss of a job, a family illness, and major relocations are just some of the problems all couples will have to deal with at some point in their marriage. The importance of flexibility in the face of upheaval cannot be stressed enough. After all, it's not how many crises befall a marriage but how a couple chooses to cope with them that determines the outcome of a relationship.

Coping with life's toughest ordeals can become much easier when a couple unites and supports one another. Unfortunately, it's precisely in times of trouble that we are prone to lose sight of the fact that we and our spouses are on the same team. Whether the problem at hand affects both partners or just one, there is a tendency to feel isolated and misunderstood by the world. Often, these feelings are simply a result of two different coping styles. One person may need more time alone, while the other may need to block out the difficulties with new activities.

At moments like these, it's imperative that you take some time to remember that anything affecting you is also affecting your spouse and that no one is immune to growing pains and adjustment difficulties. So even if you don't agree with your spouse's coping style, you can still support them by making sure they know you're on their side.

IN-LAWS AND FAMILY

One of the biggest mistakes I've seen couples make is to forget that when they marry, they are taking on their partner's entire family. Most people rarely take the time to think about all the potential issues and hazards that may crop up as a result of joining families. Of course, the decision to marry should never be decided by how much or how little a person likes their partner's family. Even so, and I cannot stress this point enough, couples must lay down some ground rules early on in the course of their relationship if they wish to avoiding running into problems down the line.

Many people think that extended family squabbling can create tension, but divorce? Never. Well, I'm here to tell you that problems with in-laws can have a devastating effect on a marriage. In my many years as a matrimonial lawyer, I have seen countless couples struggling with extended family–related issues: child rearing, holidays, cohabiting, personality conflicts, and many others that most people never even bother to consider. And although some couples can avoid in-law troubles, the majority will, to some extent, be forced to contend with keeping the peace between families.

In this chapter, we will discuss the problems associated with strained interfamilial relationships. You will learn to spot the warning signs that can alert you to the fact that your family and in-laws are causing marital discord and I will talk at length about some of the mistakes

I've seen my clients make in the process of trying to reconcile what seemed to them an irreconcilable difference. But before we get started, there is one thing I must say, and that is that there is no problem so great that it cannot be solved by two committed people who love one another.

As frustrated and powerless as you may feel in the face of extended family meddling, in-laws cannot break a marriage just as surely as they cannot make a marriage. It will be up to you to decide whether you will fight for your relationship or let it dissolve. No matter how difficult it seems or how long you've tried to make things work between you and your in-laws, there are steps you can take to salvage not only your marriage but the familial relationships that came before it.

In-Laws and Family Compatibility Assessment

Just because you are compatible with your spouse, it doesn't mean your entire family will be as well. There are so many variables that play a part in harmonious relationships between a couple and their families. Not only do you have to like your in-laws; they have to like you. And don't forget about the two sets of in-laws getting along with one another. Siblings may also play a part in your family drama. How do yours or your spouse's figure into the picture? With so many different personalities, it's a wonder how some families ever manage to sit down to the dinner table together at all. For now, try to forget about how you get along with your in-laws and focus instead on how much these people affect your marriage. To get you started, complete this exercise.

1. What were some of the positive aspects of your relationship with your in-laws at the beginning of your marriage?

   _____

2. How has your relationship with your in-laws changed with the passage of time?

   _____

3. How has your behavior and attitude toward your in-laws changed?

_____

4. Do you and your spouse ever fight about your family or in-laws?
   How often?

_____

5. If you could change one thing about your in-laws' behavior toward
   you, what would it be?

_____

6. Have you and your partner ever considered splitting up because of
   trouble with in-laws? Explain.

_____

7. Have you ever worried that your spouse could hurt your
   relationship with your family? Explain.

_____

8. Have your in-laws ever asked you to do something you were very
   uncomfortable with? Explain.

_____

9. Have you ever felt outnumbered by your spouse and his or her
   family? Explain.

_____

10. Has your spouse ever complained to you about unfair alliances between you and your family? Explain.

_____

11. Do your parents and/or siblings like your spouse? If not, are they vocal about these feelings? Explain.

_____

12. Do you feel closer to your family than to your spouse? If yes, do you think he or she is aware of this preference? Explain.

_____

13. Do you feel that your spouse's family intrudes on your time with your spouse? Explain.

_____

In-Laws and Family: Warning Signs

Warning Sign #1: Feelings of Isolation

Glenda, a 44-year-old book editor, had been married to Charlie, an electrical engineer, for over ten years before she finally realized that she was ready for a divorce. Right from the start of their relationship, Glenda was aware of the fact that Charlie was very attached to his mother. Back then, she'd thought it was a sign that he would make a good husband. Then she met the woman who'd soon become her mother-in-law.

"There was tension from the beginning," Glenda told me. "I could sense that Judy never really liked me. But it wasn't from a lack of trying. I would go out of my way to win her favor: pick up groceries, cook elaborate dinners, anything and everything to get her to like me. But whenever we were together, I couldn't help feeling that I was a third wheel.

Judy would tell all these inside jokes and make references to things that she knew I knew nothing about. I always felt that she did this on purpose. But so long as there was outward civility, I didn't feel that I really had a leg to stand on. Besides, I knew Charlie would side with her.

"I thought I had been dealing well with the situation until Judy got sick two years ago. Charlie was at the hospital all the time, but when I suggested I go, he told me that his mother wouldn't like it. He told me she was old-fashioned and only wanted family around. That's when I realized that I would never be part of the family. I was sick of feeling like the odd man out, and told Charlie as much. Of course, he didn't see it my way. He thought I was trying to sabotage their close relationship. That's when I knew I'd had enough. It was just too complicated and I had too many hurt feelings that had been waiting to erupt for too many years."

Glenda had been bottling up her feelings for so long that when they finally came out, she thought it was a sign that the marriage was failing as opposed to improving. In Glenda's case it wasn't so much a question of her in-laws but of bad timing. She waited ten years to tell her husband how she felt about his mother, and picked a time when her mother-in-law was sick in the hospital. Charlie was understandably stressed and was probably confused as to how to react to her accusations.

One thing I learned is that making the decision to divorce during times of trouble is never a good idea. I knew that Glenda's relationship with Charlie stood a better chance of surviving once the tension of his mother's illness passed. And I told Glenda as much, asking her to come back after she and Charlie had had a chance to talk things over in a calmer frame of mind.

It turned out that Charlie admitted to being a little irrational when it came to his mother, and asked Glenda to give him a chance to work things out with her. Because he had not known how frustrated and isolated Glenda had become, he had never made any efforts to dispel the tension between his wife and his mother. Once his mother was out of the hospital, Charlie began making a concerted effort to provide Glenda with a sense of belonging.

Being shut out of a spouse's family circle is one of the most frustrating and upsetting experiences a person can go through. Although many of us would never admit to this openly, the idea of being accepted into a new family, one with its own set of rules and code of conduct, can fill us with dread. All of a sudden, we're the new kid at school again and questions like, "Will they like me?" or "Will I like them?" are keeping us awake at night. And then we realize that our spouse's family is just like ours, full of flaws, contradictions, and, hopefully, good-hearted people willing to give us a chance.

Yet, there are those cases where no matter how much a person tries to get along with their in-laws, they still wind up feeling rejected and alone. Such feelings are normal, but it's important to remember that they need to be discussed before they produce any additional tension and discomfort.

Points to Ponder

1. Do you ever feel excluded from your partner and his or her family? Have you communicated your feelings to your spouse?

   _____

2. Has your partner ever expressed the feeling of not fitting in with your family? Try to recall his or her key concerns and how you addressed them.

   _____

3. Do your parents and siblings make a point to include your spouse in family gatherings and activities? If not, have you tried to consider how your partner feels?

   _____

Warning Sign #2: Bottling Up Emotions

Lorraine, a 35-year-old accountant, came into my office almost five years ago when her husband filed for a divorce. It was actually one of the first cases I had seen that so prominently featured the in-laws in the roles of marriage saboteurs. Lorraine had been married to Jerry, a mortgage broker in the city, for ten years. When the two first met, Lorraine had been living at home with her father, to whom she was very close. According to her, Jerry fell in love with her immediately, and went out of his way to make sure he'd be accepted by her father.

"It was like he was part of the family from the very beginning. He and my father would spend hours talking about this and that. I was so glad, because after my mother passed, my father had become very depressed. He stopped visiting his friends and only wanted to be home with me. After a year of dating, Jerry asked me to get married and move in with him. It was very difficult on me. So I asked Jerry if he didn't mind moving in with us for a while until we could all find a bigger place to live.

"I was very relieved when Jerry agreed to the idea. You see, I don't think I could have married Jerry if he hadn't been the kind of person who would be understanding and accepting of my relationship with my father.

"Over time, however, Jerry's relationship with my father soured. After five years of living at home, Jerry said he needed more space and privacy and began looking to move out again. Of course, I intervened and suggested that we buy a bigger space where we could all live. I had no idea that Jerry was even upset by all this until two years ago. He began to start horrible arguments with my father and me. He said that he had gone out of his way for us, and was sick of always doing the right thing. To tell you the truth, I had no idea that he felt that way. I guess he hadn't been honest with me or himself. There was nothing we could do to dispel his anger, and we decided to separate."

As evidenced by Lorraine's example, when it comes to dealing with in-laws and family, we must make every effort to avoid bottling up frustration and hostility. At first meeting, couples are on their best behavior. They are so interested in making a good impression that they often don't even take the time to form one of their own. People have been known to go overboard to please their in-laws and family. They go out of their way to make sure that they are liked, often at their own emotional and physical expense.

Over time, and by time I mean anything from a few months to a few years, people tend to become less concerned with making an impression. And if their early efforts to ingratiate themselves to their spouse's family aren't reciprocated, they can develop feelings of anger and frustration. This often happens very suddenly. They can go from being very friendly to being extremely belligerent in the blink of an eye. But even though the negative feelings seem to have developed overnight, they were probably years in the making.

Points to Ponder

1. Do you find yourself hiding your true feelings about your in-laws from your spouse?

   _____

2. Are your gestures of kindness toward your in-laws caused by appreciation of them or your need to be liked?

   _____

3. Have you ever found yourself talking negatively about your spouse's family when he or she is not around?

   _____

Warning Sign #3: Jealousy

Paul, a 44-year-old venture capitalist, had been married once before. The problem, as he explained it to me, was that his wife had been very jealous of his relationship with his mother, and refused to compromise when it came to her. With both women feuding, the situation became so unbearable that Paul actually decided it would be in everyone's best interests to end the marriage. Soon after his first divorce, he married a much younger woman, Susan, a stylist for a popular fashion magazine. They had a great relationship and were very good friends. Paul really hoped that it would work out this time.

"I guess I had been seriously burned by my first divorce because I went completely overboard trying to separate Susan and my mother. To keep both of them happy, I'd spend one weekend a month with my mother in the country and the rest of the time with Susan. I thought I had it all worked out, until Susan started complaining about my system. She resented having to give me up for a weekend. But I didn't take her very seriously.

"Suddenly, Susan became obsessed with going to see my mother with me, but the more she asked, the more I resisted. In the end, the one thing that my system had been designed to avoid—sparking Susan's jealousy—is the very thing that it wound up causing. Susan became so consumed with jealousy that it made communicating and relating to one another very difficult."

Paul had no idea that he was repeating the same mistakes over and over again. Had he gone through another divorce, he would probably have found the very same problem resurfacing in his third marriage. Paul didn't need a divorce; he needed to change how he related to his wife and his mother. By keeping Susan and his mother apart, he was preventing them from forming a bond that might have been to everyone's advantage. I knew that he would have to give Susan and his mother a chance to be together in order to fix the situation. So I suggested that he give them a chance to get to know one another before filing for a divorce.

Although Susan and her mother-in-law didn't become best friends overnight, they did find enough common ground to be able to coexist harmoniously. Both Susan and Paul felt much more at ease with their roles in the family, and are still together to this very day.

A certain degree of jealousy is expected in any relationship. After all, we all like to think that our spouse loves us and that we are their number one priority. There will always be a certain amount of competition between your spouse and your family members. It's only natural. Your parents also experience some degree of this emotion, even if everything seems fine on the surface. So although jealousy is entirely natural, it must not be allowed to remain unchecked. Never ignore your spouse's feelings of jealousy, because although all may seem right as rain at first, a little jealousy can snowball into a great deal of conflict and heartache in the end.

Signs of Jealousy

Determining whether your spouse is jealous of your relationship with your family is not difficult, provided you know what signs to look for:

- trying to monopolize your attention during family outings

- not asking your family questions or engaging them in conversations

- grilling you about your relationship with your family

- pointing out flaws in how your family treats you

- finding alternatives to spending time with your family

In-Laws and Family: Crimes and Misdemeanors

Crime and Misdemeanor #1: Taking Sides

Eleanor and Jeremy had been married for only three years. It was Jeremy who filed for divorce and sought out my services. A hard-working man, Jeremy had built his thriving contracting business up from scratch. He had the look of a man who had had a lot of struggle in his life, but as he told me, "Nothing was more difficult than getting along with my in-laws.

"When Eleanor and I first married, I noticed she had a tendency to side with her parents. If I suggested a drive in the country and her mother suggested having dinner first, we would have dinner first. But I loved Eleanor so much that it didn't matter, or at least I thought it wouldn't. I also hoped that my relationship with her parents would improve. The problem was that they came from a different, much wealthier, background. My business was just getting off the ground, and I don't think they believed that I could support Eleanor on my own.

"Fortunately, we lived over an hour's drive from her family. Of course, I did have to survive the holidays, but I knew it was only a matter of time until we would return home. Eventually, as my business began to grow, Eleanor's family wanted to have an even bigger role in our life. I think they were a little disturbed by the fact that I was finally out of debt and didn't need their support.

"That's when our marriage took a turn for the worse. Eleanor's mother began calling every minute of the day. Everything from where we would vacation to designing our apartment was suddenly an issue. And the worst of it was that Eleanor would crumble in her mother's presence. She simply couldn't stand up to her, even when the issue was clearly our personal business.

"When I suggested that Eleanor take a more decisive tone with her mother, Eleanor turned around and told me that her mother was usually right in all matters, and she valued her opinion above mine. Maybe she didn't exactly say it in those words, but from that day on, I knew that I was in second place, and that's something I just could not live with."

In times of conflict between your spouse and your parents, or you and your in-laws, taking sides can add a very destructive element to an already volatile situation. One of the major contributors to conflict with in-laws is the fact that the former alliances have been broken down and replaced with a new one—the relationship between you and your partner.

I have seen many couples make the mistake of becoming too caught up in their private family feuds. Often, they complain about being in a no-win situation. What I'm here to tell you is that defending your family to the detriment of your spouse, or vice versa, will always result in a no-win situation. It is important for you to learn to play both sides of the white picket fence. The secret to becoming an impartial observer is listening. If you can do that, you will be the one everyone comes to for advice and mediation when push comes to shove.

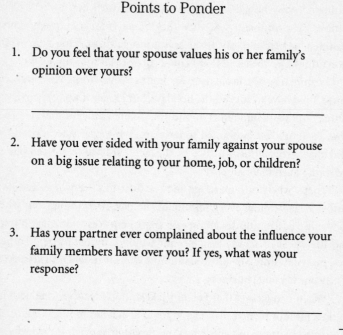

Points to Ponder

1. Do you feel that your spouse values his or her family's opinion over yours?

    _____

2. Have you ever sided with your family against your spouse on a big issue relating to your home, job, or children?

    _____

3. Has your partner ever complained about the influence your family members have over you? If yes, what was your response?

    _____

Crime and Misdemeanor #2: Sabotaging Family Relations

Dennis and Eva met while they were pursuing their MBAs at Columbia College Business School. From what Dennis told me, both of them were extremely ambitious. The relationship blossomed and only a year later, the two were reciting their marital vows in front of their families. Dennis and Eva had no problems when it came to forging solid relationships with their in-laws, but there was already some obvious tension between Eva and Dennis's brother Greg.

"Greg and I were extremely close. We even lived together up to the day I got married. Of course, Greg was not happy to see me go, but, like any good brother, he supported me in my decision. When Eva and I first started going out, I knew that she and Greg wouldn't hit it off. He was always very artistic and had dreams of opening up his own art gallery someday. Well, ever the pragmatist, Eva thought he was a first-rate slacker. She didn't really agree with him on anything, being so level-headed and business oriented. The thing was that I really believed the two of them would be able to get along someday. I figured that if Greg and I, being the complete opposites that we were, could get along, then Eva would also eventually come around. But nothing worked. Throughout our five years together, Eva would criticize Greg nonstop.

"The problems really became worse when Greg lost the lease on our old apartment. He was having a hard time finding a job he was comfortable with, and really wanted to take his time to find just the right position. Eva, of course, thought that he wasn't even looking for a job. But I knew that this was not the case. One day, Greg asked me if he could move in with me and Eva for a couple of weeks, while he found a cheaper place to live. I knew that Eva would react negatively, but I could never have expected the tantrum that she threw. That's when I saw her for the person she really was.

"Instead of feeling sympathy for Greg, she demanded that I tell him to find another place to live. I knew then that Greg would never forgive me for turning my back on him, so I made a choice, which was much easier when I realized that the problems in our marriage had nothing to do with me or my family, but with Eva's complete lack of sensitivity and consideration."

No situation is loaded with quite so much potential for disaster as one in which a person deliberately creates a rift between their spouse and their spouse's parents and/or siblings. Most people who engage in this behavior have a million rationalizations to justify themselves. But no matter what reasons in-laws and family may have given someone to dislike them—whether it be meddling, criticism, or even invasion of privacy—nothing can justify a deliberate attempt to sever family relations. Even if a partner is successful in loosening the family ties that bind his or her spouse to their family, their spouse will never be able to forgive them. In the vast majority of such cases, the outcome is not only a breakdown of the in-law relationship, but the marriage as well.

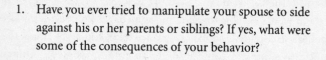

Points to Ponder

1. Have you ever tried to manipulate your spouse to side against his or her parents or siblings? If yes, what were some of the consequences of your behavior?

    _____

2. Do you feel that your spouse supports your relationship with your family?

    _____

3. How often do you make negative comments to your partner about his or her family? If frequently, consider what would happen if the situation was reversed.

    _____

Crime and Misdemeanor #3: Showing Disrespect

Moira, a 45-year-old social worker, came to me to file for a divorce from her husband, David, a middle-aged computer programmer. The two had been married for over twenty years, and from the look on Moira's face, as she described the events leading up to her decision, I could tell that the idea of getting a divorce had been brewing for quite some time.

As it turned out, Moira had remained with David purely for the sake of their children. She'd gotten pregnant very early into the marriage and had no idea about David's temper until it was too late. Naturally, Moira's mother worried about her daughter and took an intense dislike to David as soon as his true colors became apparent.

"David couldn't stand knowing that my mother disliked him. Funny as it seems, he prided himself on being a likable guy. In the first ten years of our marriage, I would let his occasional outbursts at my mother slide. I thought that if I kept them far apart, she would never have to deal with him. But when my father passed away a few years ago, she moved to New York to be near me.

"Life became extremely difficult from that point on. My two daughters had gone off to college, and I began spending more and more time with my mother. Unfortunately, David's path began crossing with my mother's more and more often, and he became increasingly hostile in his dealings with her. Instead of hiding his hostility, he voiced his anger and his presence in our home began to feel even more oppressive than usual. His behavior was simply inexcusable. One night, after a big fight, my mother stormed out of our apartment. But instead of watching her leave, I packed my bags and followed suit. It was the best decision I had ever made. The only thing I was confused about was why it had taken me so long to leave in the first place."

Moira was right. Insulting and verbally abusing one's in-laws is simply inexcusable. There is no rationale for hurting or insulting the people your spouse cares for. Harboring some negative feelings toward in-laws is normal, but voicing those feelings without making any attempt at tact, decorum, and common civility can have detrimental effects on your marriage.

Points to Ponder

1. Have you or your spouse ever directly insulted each other's family members? How frequently does this go on?

   _____

2. Have your parents ever complained about the way your spouse treats them?

   _____

3. Do you ever argue about how your partner treats your family after they leave? If yes, do you think your spouse has any intention of changing?

In-Laws and Family: Effecting a Reconciliation

Reconciliation #1: Outline Expectations

Lynn, a 53-year-old optometrist, sought out my services before divorcing her second husband. There was nothing especially remarkable about the divorce itself, save the fact that Lynn came into my office with her ex-mother-in-law, Doris, with whom she'd grown very close during her marriage to her first husband, Doris's son. They were so close that I couldn't resist asking how they had forged such a strong bond. Knowing how many of my clients had struggled unsuccessfully with in-law–related issues, I just had to find out about this wonderful and rather startling relationship.

"Oh, we've always been close," Lynn replied with a wave of her hand.

"Not as I recall," disagreed Doris. "Lynn doesn't like to talk about some of the problems we had when she and my son first got engaged. Believe me, it wasn't always like this. Lynn and I could bicker about anything, until, one day and quite by accident, we ran into each other on the street. We had both been shopping and decided to take a break for lunch. It was during that one afternoon that we became good friends.

"We talked about what was bothering us, and really came to an understanding about what we each expected out of our relationship. All she wanted was some independence and respect. And, of course, I wanted to stay close to my son and have some involvement in their lives. We both agreed to each other's requests. After that brief discussion, our relationship even exceeded my expectations. I never thought that we would grow so close. But we did, so much so, in fact, that my son was sometimes jealous of our friendship."

Early in the book, I suggested that all couples outline their expectations of one another early on in their marriage. However, I never said that you should stop there. It is critical that you have a discussion with both sets of in-laws and all siblings as well, because no matter how difficult it is to believe at first, your new relatives will have a significant impact on your marriage.

Our expectations for everything from our marriages to our jobs, friends, and in-laws have a lot to do with our hopes and desires and very little to do with what others are prepared to give. Not only that, but we become so wrapped up in what we want that we never really take the time to figure out what is expected of us. By showing your in-laws and family members that you care to listen to them and find out what needs they are interested in fulfilling, you will be one step closer to forging a relationship that both you and your spouse's family can live with.

Points to Ponder

1. Have you ever thought about what you could do to make your in-laws more accommodating?

   _____

2. Do you think your in-laws are aware of what you expect of them?

   _____

3. Do you think your expectations of your in-laws are realistic?

   _____

Reconciliation #2: Bow Out Gracefully

Jane, a promising young artist, and Paul, a 46-year-old corporate trainer, had been married for seven years when Paul began having problems with Jane's parents. It all started when her father's company encountered financial difficulty.

Jane had long been a source of emotional support for her father. But their time together was cut to a fraction when she moved to New York. When she married Paul, Jane's opportunities to see her father dwindled to monthly visits that always included Paul. Since her father didn't want to reveal his company's woes to Paul, Jane had a very hard time talking to her father with her husband around.

"When I suggested that Paul stay behind while I visited my family alone, he was insulted and demanded to know what he'd done to make my parents dislike him so. Finally, I told Paul what was happening with my father's company. But instead of letting the situation settle down, he demanded to get involved in all aspects of my father's financial problems. He was overconfident to say the least, but I knew he just wanted to help. My father, however, did not want Paul to get involved. I think it was a matter of pride. In fact, he was mad at me for telling Paul before consulting with him first.

"At that point, I decided to tell Paul everything, thinking he would understand and just let me visit my family on my own. When he didn't agree and began sending me e-mails outlining ways to help my father, I had just had enough. It's one thing to want to help, but quite another to be so tactless, inconsiderate, and controlling that you hurt everyone around you."

It was clear to me that Paul was very insecure about his position in the family, and I asked Jane to consider the situation from his point of view. Despite his inability to give her family space, Paul was basically a decent guy with good intentions. Of course, he would need to learn how to give his wife the space she needed to help her family, but this was definitely a case of someone simply trying too hard to fit in.

When I talked to Jane again a few weeks later, I asked her to consider talking to Paul with a mediator to explain exactly what it was that was making her want to get a divorce. It turned out that Paul had been having a difficult time believing that someone wouldn't want help in Jane's father's position. He thought Jane was simply being polite by not trying to involve him, but he soon realized just how grave the situation had become. Once he finally heard Jane out and understood what she needed from the relationship, it was easier for him to take a step back when it came to his in-laws.

Meddling in your spouse's relationship with their family or neglecting to give your spouse and their parents some space can backfire. Of course, it's very easy to lose sight of the fine line that lies between spending quality time and becoming an imposition. Your in-laws and spouse may be overly polite and feel that they need to include you in every activity. And although they probably enjoy your company, there might be times when all they want is to have some time alone with their son or daughter.

If you stop to think about it, spending another Sunday with the extended family is probably not high on your list of favorite activities. If you feel that there are things you'd rather be doing, then it's quite likely that your spouse's family feels the same. Do you feel obligated to escort your spouse to every family get-together, or can you honestly say that there's nothing you'd like better? If obligation plays any kind of role in your relationship with the in-laws, it may be time to cut back on the time you spend at family reunions—the feeling may be mutual.

Points to Ponder

1. Do you attend every family function with your spouse?

   _____

2. Have you ever accompanied your spouse to a family event out of obligation?

   _____

3. How do you think your in-laws would react if you were
    absent?

_____

Reconciliation #3: Learn to Mediate

Thomas, a 48-year-old corporate executive, came into my office to discuss getting a divorce from Gwen, his wife of ten years. He was extremely unhappy about the prospect of not being with his wife, but was confused about how to handle a situation that had recently arisen. Mostly, he looked tired and agitated. Of course, I could understand why he was under so much strain. It seems that his father was terminally ill and had appointed Thomas's older brother as his successor.

"My two brothers and I always knew this day would come, but no one could have known that it would create so much bad blood in the family. Since I was the middle child, my older brother, Robert, was chosen to head the company. Of course, he didn't have any of the experience I had, and I was legitimately concerned about the future of the company. So I began trying to persuade my father to change his mind.

"When Gwen found out what was happening, she immediately jumped to my defense. Whenever we would all get together, she would start lobbying on my behalf, talking about how successful and effective I'd been in my role. I couldn't blame her, at first. She was just looking out for me. But after a while, it started to look to everyone like I was training her to say all those things. I tried talking to her about it, asking her to restrain herself. Yet, the more I begged her, the more adamant she became about making sure that I got what she thought I deserved."

Gwen's interference was symptomatic of a much bigger issue. She'd always pressured and motivated Robert into great accomplishment, and he'd thanked her for it. At this point, however, Gwen's dismissal of Robert's feelings, and those of his family members, for the sake of his career advancement looked selfish.

In that situation, Robert didn't need Gwen to fight. Instead, he needed her to take on the role of mediator. Since he had to work through his own issues with the family business, it would have been much more helpful had Gwen tried to play the impartial observer rather than someone who was so personally involved in the situation.

Robert had tried talking to Gwen about her behavior, but that had only put her on the defensive. In her mind, she was simply looking out for her husband's welfare. Knowing that Gwen was a caring person and that she wanted to make the relationship work, Robert gave the marriage more time so he and Gwen could see a counselor. It was during their therapy sessions that Robert was finally able to communicate that he wanted Gwen to diffuse the conflict within his family rather than fan the flames. After months of working on their personal issues, the couple decided to give the marriage another chance.

Simply put, selfishness has no place within family conflict where the primary objective is to do what's best for the group, not the individual. So, if you have any hope of getting along with your spouse's in-laws and siblings, you will probably end up having to reconcile yourself to the role of mediator. Having met hundreds of couples who are unable to make it work with their in-laws, I know how much damage an "us versus the rest of the family" attitude can wreak. Distancing yourself from the conflict and focusing on solutions and compromises is the only way to maintain old relationships while fortifying new ones.

Steps to Successful Mediation

Before you take on the difficult but rewarding role of mediator, you should understand the importance of remaining unbiased and objective. No matter how much you want to interject and impose your own view on the proceedings, everyone will be better served if you try to listen to both sides and foster a mutually satisfying resolution. The following steps will help you accomplish this goal:

1. Listen carefully to both sides.

2. Ask each side to clarify their position to the other.

3. Ensure mutual understanding by asking each side to repeat the other's position.

4. Try to identify the hidden issues that are not being discussed.

5. Figure out where you can compromise and which points are non-negotiable.

6. Address issues of yelling and sarcasm by asking the offenders to modify their speech.

7. Encourage both sides to offer solutions rather than criticism.

8. Seal the deal in writing: Keep a record of meeting points and resolutions.

In-Laws and Family: Closing Argument

One of the most difficult things about problems with in-laws and family is that the issues affect a lot more people than just you and your spouse. Whenever two families merge, there is bound to be friction at first. That is almost an inevitability. Just because you and your spouse love one another doesn't mean your in-laws and siblings will share your positive feelings. How you and your spouse cope with that tension is what will make the difference, because in the end, that's the thing that will determine the stability of your union and the way your loved ones treat your marriage down the line.

The best way to prevent future problems with in-laws is to figure out what works for the family early on. If your in-laws have a tendency to meddle, let them know from the beginning where you stand. If you feel your in-laws are a bad influence on the children, make sure you supervise all their visits. By taking simple precautions early on in the marriage and setting patterns and parameters, you will prevent major problems from happening later on.

Finally, always make an effort to show your in-laws and family members that you care about their needs. Show them that you're not a threat and you will be one step closer to forging a solid relationship based on respect and mutual consideration.

A FINAL CLOSING STATEMENT

Just by reading this book, you have shown a commitment to making your marriage work. By taking the time to analyze your marriage and learning about the do's and don'ts of successful and unsuccessful matches, you have begun to grasp the key to building a solid foundation for your family, which is the willingness and determination to work things out even when a solution is not readily apparent.

Sometimes, it is only by considering divorce that we actually begin to appreciate and value the relationship we have with our spouse. I say this because after thirty-some years of practicing matrimonial law, I have become even more committed to the institution of marriage. Years of listening to sad stories about broken families have not turned me against marriage—just the opposite.

It is precisely because I have heard so many clients recount their marital woes that I am able to maintain my optimism. Every story, every single mistake, every tragic flaw that I see and hear in the process of representing my clients reminds me of just how human and fallible we all are. It also reminds me of just how similar we all are and that by listening to others, we can avoid their mistakes and build happy unions that will see us well into our golden years. If I've learned anything it is that all of us will go through the same rituals, the same discontent, the same issues at some point in our marriages. For some reason, that thought gives me comfort, and I beseech you to take comfort in it as well whenever you feel alone in the world and helpless in the face of life's challenges.

We are all trying to make the best of our marriages and maintain the love and affection that compelled us to take our vows in the first place. Whether we're high-profile celebrities or just hard-working, everyday people, all of us, at some point in our lives, will find ourselves face to face with the choices that can save or break our marriages. Although many of my clients are wealthy and well-known in their respective fields, their stories are not unique to their fancy Park Avenue apartments and polished boardrooms. They are just people who try to make the most of their lives and often fail in the process. I have learned from them, and so can you.

It is important that we learn from everyone who has lost in the marriage game and try to understand the factors contributing to their divorces. As a matrimonial lawyer who has seen thousands of clients come through my office, I have been in the fortunate position of being able to learn about which behaviors and attitudes make marriages work and which are destructive to the relationship. And what amazes me most is that from the many cases I have heard, there are only a few principles to extract, a few common lessons to learn. I have found that the principles of a successful marriage are not that complicated, and that, sometimes, a few simple changes can be all it takes to revive a failing marriage.

By following the simple rules I have laid out in this book, you will be fast on your way to avoiding the most common pitfalls of marriage. If you find yourself committing any of the crimes and misdemeanors or spotting the common warning signs in your own marriage, you should not waste any time in applying the reconciliation methods outlined at the end of each chapter. The only danger to your marriage is letting problems go unresolved and unnoticed. All couples must grapple with the same issues and concerns. The only difference is that some couples take the necessary steps to address and solve their conflicts while others wait until it is too late—in other words, until divorce is their only option.

Putting your union on automatic pilot may be convenient enough when you have your job and children to balance, but the problems that will collect in the process will eventually remind you of your error. This book was written to help you understand that divorce does not have to be your only recourse. If you follow the steps and guidelines I have out-lined, you will learn that the key to avoiding stepping into my office is to remain vigilant and aware of your marriage's progress, even when you have a million other priorities that seem important at the time.

What's clear to me and what should be clear to you after reading this book is that no marriage is half as complicated as a divorce. No matter how difficult you think your situation is now, you will find that it is nothing in comparison to your typical divorce proceedings.

The most important thing is to listen to your spouse, your friends, and your family—and you have already started doing this. Make contin-uous efforts to learn about relationships and seek counseling if needed. Learn from each other as you have done from the people in this book. Learn from their mistakes so as not to let them become your own.

ACKNOWLEDGMENTS

I would like to thank Joni Evans for making this book happen; Elina Furman for helping me write this book; Mitchell Ivers for his patience and superb editing; my partners at Morrison Cohen Singer & Weinstein, who gave me the time to do this; and my assistant, Shelli Rosenthal, who keeps everything on track.